Images courtesy of:
Dreamstime, Hobbycraft, Thinkstock;

Copy Editor Juliette O'Neill

**CAT NO: SON0581
ISBN: 978-1-915343-35-2**

Made in the UAE.

The Compact Beginner's Guide to

Quilting &
Patchwork

Welcome to

The Compact Beginner's Guide to

Quilting & Patchwork

Recent years have seen a positive boom when it comes to homecrafts, from using yarns in knitwear to making your own patchwork creations.

In **The Compact Beginner's Guide to Quilting & Patchwork**, you'll find everything you require to start completing your own patchwork projects, from the basic tools you will need through all the best techniques and block patterns so you can create your own ideal quilt. There's no limit to what you can create. Following our step-by-step tutorials you can discover all the skills you need to craft the most beautiful projects. Once you've learnt the skills and techniques, we've provided you with some great starter projects, including a fun circuit-board design, an ice-cream quilt perfect for the beach, and a tote bag ideal for running to the shops.

Go forth and get quilting!

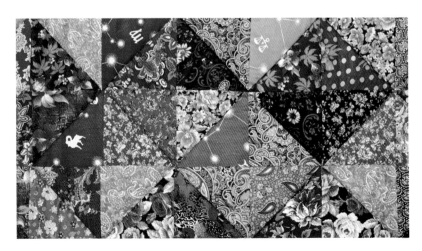

Contents

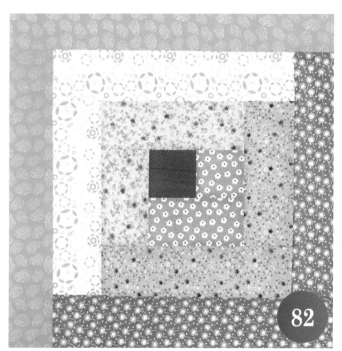

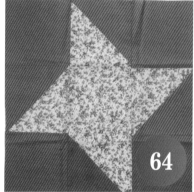

Tools & materials

Getting started

Tools & materials

Everything you need to know to get started with quilting

"Here, we will guide you through the basics of your machine, from the main functions involved and how they can be useful"

Quilting tools

There are several steps in putting together your new quilt, and each requires its own set of tools. Here's a run-down of the essentials you'll need to get started

When you go to the haberdashery to pick out the fabric you want to use in your quilt, you'll need to make decisions like the colour palette and patterns you want for your project. But before you get to this stage, which is arguably one of the most exciting in the quilt-making process, it's important to understand all the different parts of a piece of fabric, and how they can affect the way that you work with it and what the finished result will look like. So when it actually comes to picking the ones you want to work with from the huge variety available, you'll know which will be most suitable for your project.

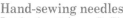

Hand-sewing needles
Even though most of your quilt will be sewn together with a sewing machine, needles are always handy to have around. A variety pack will have a selection of eye sizes and needle length/width, offering the most versatility.

Magnetic pincushion
This handy tool will pick up any loose pins or needles just by moving it near them. It will also hold pins for a nifty way to store them.

Safety pins
As well as being used to pull elastic through casings, safety pins are a good replacement for straight pins, should you need them.

Needle threader
If you're not the best at passing thread through the eye of a needle, this compact tool can save many hours of frustration and reams of frayed thread.

Pins and needles
You will use lots and lots of these while making a quilt, so it's important to stock up. Ones with glass heads are best, as there's no risk of them melting during pressing.

Stuffed pincushion
Push your pins into one of these to keep them safe and make them easy to grab. If your sewing skills are a bit rusty, making your own pincushion is a quick and simple practice project.

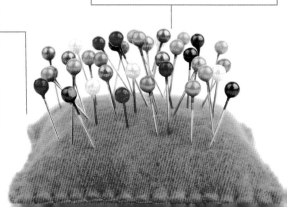

"It's important to understand all the different parts of a piece of fabric"

Measuring tools

Seam gauge
Also called a sewing gauge, this small ruler with a marker is handy for measuring out even hems or pleats.

Plastic ruler
An extra long and wide ruler is best to use when quilting, as it will keep the fabric underneath it still, but a standard ruler is also fine to use in a pinch, as long as it is clear so you can see where you're working.

Flexible tape measure
As these are typically much longer than plastic rulers, they are useful for measuring larger things, for example the layout of your finished quilt to check it is the desired size.

Cloth-marking pencil
Make sure that anything you use to mark your fabric will wash out later. Pencils are easy to use and keep sharp, but you could also use tailor's chalk or a water-erasable marker.

Self-healing cutting mat
This kind of mat will prevent you from marking your furniture when you are cutting your fabric, but it also comes with a ruler printed on top. This will enable you to cut perfect edges and corners when you line your fabric up on it.

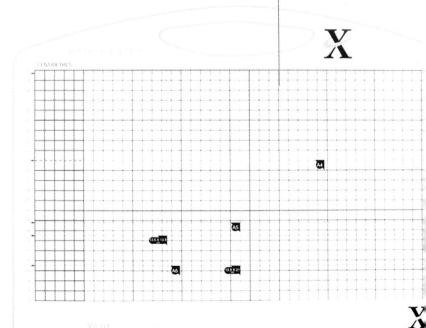

Cutting tools

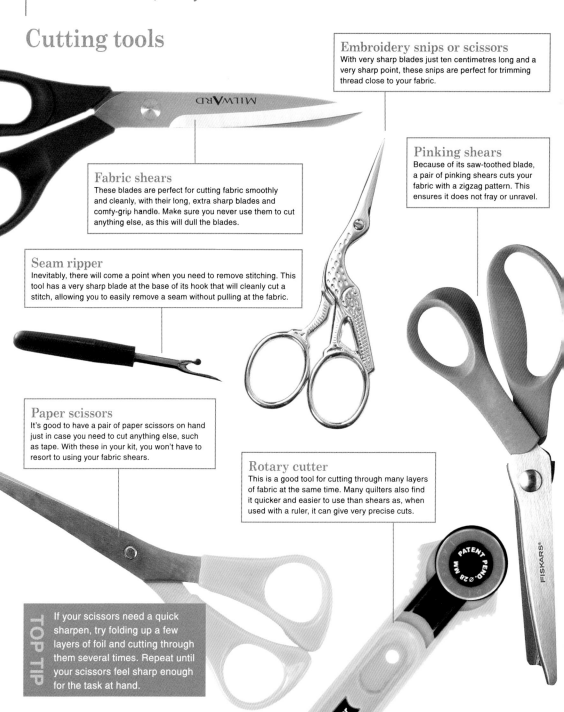

Embroidery snips or scissors
With very sharp blades just ten centimetres long and a very sharp point, these snips are perfect for trimming thread close to your fabric.

Fabric shears
These blades are perfect for cutting fabric smoothly and cleanly, with their long, extra sharp blades and comfy-grip handle. Make sure you never use them to cut anything else, as this will dull the blades.

Pinking shears
Because of its saw-toothed blade, a pair of pinking shears cuts your fabric with a zigzag pattern. This ensures it does not fray or unravel.

Seam ripper
Inevitably, there will come a point when you need to remove stitching. This tool has a very sharp blade at the base of its hook that will cleanly cut a stitch, allowing you to easily remove a seam without pulling at the fabric.

Paper scissors
It's good to have a pair of paper scissors on hand just in case you need to cut anything else, such as tape. With these in your kit, you won't have to resort to using your fabric shears.

Rotary cutter
This is a good tool for cutting through many layers of fabric at the same time. Many quilters also find it quicker and easier to use than shears as, when used with a ruler, it can give very precise cuts.

TOP TIP
If your scissors need a quick sharpen, try folding up a few layers of foil and cutting through them several times. Repeat until your scissors feel sharp enough for the task at hand.

Pressing tools

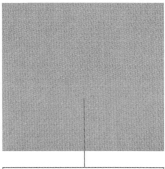

Sleeve board
This small version of an ironing board is ideal for pressing small areas or seams. It can easily be set up in your workspace when there isn't enough space to get the full-size ironing board out.

Pressing cloth
Placing a thin piece of cotton cloth in between your fabric and iron when pressing will help prevent residue transferring from the iron to quilt and vice versa, and also prevent iron shine.

Wooden point turner
Just one of the versatile wooden point turner's uses is finger pressing. Pushing the curved end along a fabric fold will give a nice, crisp crease.

TOP TIP
Other tools that aren't essential but you might want to invest in include thimbles, pattern weights and some storage to keep all your new things in.

Ironing board
An ironing board provides the best surface on which to press your quilt, as it is completely flat and designed for such a purpose, ensuring you won't burn or melt any other work surfaces.

Steam iron
The best irons for pressing come with a steam function and the option to vary the temperature. Most often, steam will be essential when pressing.

Anatomy of a sewing machine

Understanding your machine and how it works is key to unlocking your creative potential

The first thing you will want to do when you start quilting is to get to know your tools, most specifically your sewing machine. Here, we will guide you through the basics of your machine, from what the main functions involved and how they can be useful to you in your quilting projects. Each sewing machine varies, so giving a complete guide can be quite difficult. While we can point out the main features of most machines, you may find that this differs from the machine that you have. In these instances, we suggest that you refer to your own individual operating manual as this will be specific to your own machine.

TOP TIP

Make sure that you have a copy of your own sewing machine's manual, just incase you need to know a little more detail about how to operate it!

"Each sewing machine varies, so giving a complete guide can be quite difficult"

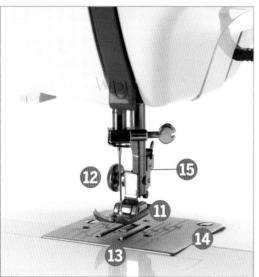

Know your machine

Your machine will likely be different, but the main features will be similar and recognisable.

1. Power button
2. Foot controller/power cord jack
3. Handwheel
4. Take-up lever
5. Tension dial
6. Thread guide
7. Stitch selection
8. Bobbin winder

9. Reverse stitch
10. Presser foot lever
11. Presser foot
12. Needle threader
13. Bobbin housing
14. Throat plate
15. Thread cutter

Machine needles

Kit up your machine with the right kind of needles

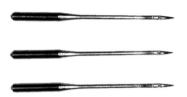

Universal needles

Standard for most machines, universal needles are the most common type and can be used on a range of materials. They come in a variety of sizes depending on the weight of the material you're sewing, and are best used with cotton, polyester or silk threads.

Twin needles

Great for decorative stitches, twin needles can also be used for creating a pin-tucking effect. Be sure to stitch slowly, however, as they're much more intricate than other needles and care needs to be taken when using them.

Ballpoint needles

Featuring a slightly more rounded tip than other needles, the ball point needle pushes weaves in chunkier fabric apart, which makes them ideal for use with knitted fabrics. Unlike the ball-point needle, sharper needles tend to cut through fabric, which can result in rips and laddering.

Microtex needles

On the flip side, Microtex needles are notoriously sharp, which makes it much easier for them to cut through densely woven materials. This type of needle is ideal for use with silks, foils and other delicate materials that you may choose.

Replace your needle

Not every machine comes with the needle already in place, so make sure you know how to get set to stitch with our handy guide.

01 Reach the needle

First of all, you'll need to remove or lower the foot that's currently on your machine to access the needle. Next, using a small screwdriver or your hand, unscrew the needle clamp to loosen the needle.

02 Replace the needle

You should be able to pull out the needle easily. Be aware of where the flat side of the needle sits and then place a fresh needle in line with the flat sides. Once it's in, retighten the screw and replace the foot on your sewing machine.

Unscrew the needle clamp

Machine feet

With a range of feet for your sewing machine available, it can be tricky to choose the right set for your machine

Zigzag foot
The default foot that comes with your machine, the zigzag foot is an all-purpose and pleasingly versatile option for straight or zigzag stitches. It's also a good option for decorative stitches.

Monogramming foot
Wider than the standard zigzag foot, the monogramming foot provides more visibility and a broader motion range to create decorative monograms or appliqué.

Button-fitting foot
Take the time out of attaching buttons with this handy foot. The foot is capable of sewing on two-hole or four-hole buttons onto garments, but be sure to set your zigzag stitch's length to zero.

Cording foot
Also known as the multi-cord foot, this foot allows you to add a piping effect to your projects very easily. It can be used with either a straight stitch or a zigzag stitch, and if you want an invisible sewing result then be sure to use monofilament thread.

Overlock foot
This foot is great for finishing the edges of fabrics or reinforcing raw edges. You can also create a rolled hem using the overlock foot and a bit of patience.

Zipper foot
The zipper foot is fairly obvious from its name — it enables you to sew close to zip teeth in order to create a neat and tidy seam, without having to apply pressure to the zip with the pressing mechanism. The foot can be adjusted for both sides of the machine, too.

Blind hem foot
This foot is perfect for creating barely-there hems on your projects, which hides the stitches on both sides of the material. A guide on the foot ensures the stitch is kept at a certain distance from the hem.

Buttonhole foot
The buttonhole foot takes the pain out of stitching button holes, as you simply place the button into the foot to set the size, then let the machine automatically do all the hard work. If you're lucky enough to have a newer advanced machine, it may be able to memorise the buttonhole size for future projects until reprogrammed.

Invisible zipper foot
Built with grooves to line up with the teeth of the zip, the invisible zipper foot creates seemingly not-there stitches along zips, while hiding it all. This foot is perfect for clothing protects or cushions.

Adjust the tension

Knowing how to adjust your tension is pivotal for your stitches appearing to be correct when you are sewing with your machine. We'll take you through what you need to do to get it right

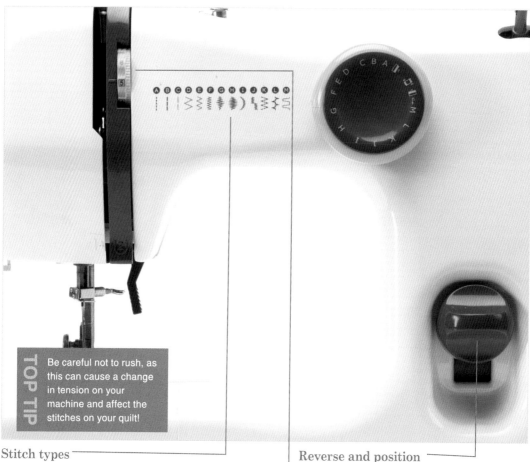

> **TOP TIP**
> Be careful not to rush, as this can cause a change in tension on your machine and affect the stitches on your quilt!

Stitch types

Different machines will have a different array of stitches available to you. Some will have the basics, singular short and long stitches and the zigzag capabilities but some will come with the most complex looking combinations you won't understand how your machine can possibly do it with one needle and a bobbin!

To set the stitches, you simply need to select the number with the buttons (or in some cases a wheel) and the machine will do the work for you. You may need to adjust the tension for different types of stitches, and you can adjust the length and width of each of them.

If you are unsure, it is best to refer to the user manual for your specific machine, as this is vary massively per each product.

Reverse and position

These will vary per machine, some have a button while others will have a lever. Likewise, the needle position and speed controls will be different depending on your machine. Some will only have speed controls based upon how light or hard you press the pedal.

Tension dial

To change the tension, you will need to turn your dial. This will vary per machine but the higher the number you set it to, the looser the stitch will be.

Fabric defined

At first glance, a piece of fabric might seem rather basic. However, understanding its complexities can help you when it comes to choosing the best ones for your quilt

When you go to the haberdashery to pick out the fabric you want to use in your quilt, you'll need to make decisions on matters like the colour palette and the patterns you want for your project. But before you get to this stage, which is arguably one of the most exciting in the quilt-making process, it's important to understand all the different parts of a piece of fabric, and how they can affect the way that you work with it and what the finished result will look like. So when it actually comes to picking the ones you want to work with from the huge variety available, you'll know which will be most suitable for your project.

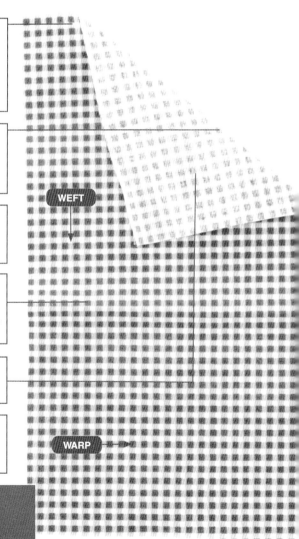

Selvedge
The self-finished edge of the fabric prevents the piece from unravelling or fraying. The selvedge will be thicker than the rest of the fabric and may not be patterned. Most selvedges will be narrow, but some could be quite wide depending on how the material was manufactured. It is not uncommon for a fabric selvedge to be discarded by sewers, as it is often unusable.

Bias
The bias grain is the line of thread that is at a 45-degree angle from the selvedge. Find it by folding your piece of fabric diagonally in half with the selvedge at the bottom. Pieces of fabric cut on the bias generally have a bit more stretch in them, and may fray less.

Weft threads
These are the threads that are drawn over and under the warp threads during weaving. As they do not need to be pulled and stretched like the warp threads, they may be made of slightly weaker material.

Right side
What is referred to as the right side of the fabric is the finished side, and the one you'll want to be visible on your quilt. If your fabric is printed, it should be easy to tell which is the right side, as it should be clearer and brighter.

Wrong side
The underside of the fabric is called the wrong side, as it will make up the part of the quilt you want to be hidden.

Warp threads
These are the lengthwise threads of woven fabric, which run parallel to the selvedge. During the weaving process, they are the threads that are held in place on a loop or frame.

WEFT

WARP

"The self-finished edge prevents the piece from unravelling"

Yardage	Inches	cm
⅛	4½	11.5
¼	9	23
⅓	12	30.5
⅜	13½	34.25
½	18	45.75
⅝	22½	57
⅔	24	61
¾	27	68.5
⅞	31½	80

Yardage conversion chart

Fabric comes in many different widths, and it's likely that, if you're following a pattern, it may only specify how many yards of fabric you need for one width. If the fabric you want to use comes in a different width, you will need either more or less yards of it than the pattern calls for. Use this handy chart to find out how much you'll need to get.

1 yard = 36in (91.5cm)

TOP TIP
It's always better to have more fabric than not enough. If you're even a little uncertain about how many yards you need, add an extra half.

Fabric width	35-36in	39in	41in	44-45in	50in	52-54in	60in
Yardage	1 ¾	1 ½	1 ½	1 ⅜	1 ¼	1 ⅛	1
	2	1 ¾	1 ¾	1 ⅝	1 ½	1 ⅜	1 ¼
	2 ¼	2	2	1 ¾	1 ⅝	1 ½	1 ⅜
	2 ½	2 ¼	2 ¼	2 ⅛	1 ¾	1 ¾	1 ⅝
	2 ⅞	2 ½	2 ½	2 ¼	2	1 ⅞	1 ¾
	3 ⅛	2 ¾	2 ¾	2 ½	2 ¼	2	1 ⅞
	3 ⅜	3	2 ⅞	2 ¾	2 ⅜	2 ¼	2
	3 ¾	3 ¼	3 ⅛	2 ⅞	2 ⅝	2 ⅜	2 ¼
	4 ¼	3 ½	3 ⅜	3 ⅛	2 ¾	2 ⅝	2 ⅜
	4 ¾	4	3 ⅞	3 ⅝	3 ¼	2 ⅞	2 ¾
	5	4 ¼	4 ⅛	3 ⅞	3 ⅜	3 ⅛	2 ⅞

Fabric types

With so many fabrics to choose from for your project, you need to consider what exactly you want to achieve before selecting your material

From cotton to corduroy and silk to soft knit, there are so many materials to pick from, and the choice can certainly be a hard one if you're new to sewing. While achieving a spectacular end result is the ultimate aim, you don't want to fall at the first hurdle by picking a fabric that's too tricky to work with — after all, some materials work better for quilting than others. If you're a more experienced sewer, however, you might want to give the more complex fabrics a whirl...

Cotton

Available in block colours or in a printed pattern, pure cotton is a favourite for quilting. Non-stretch, easy to sew and available in fun prints, cotton can be pre-washed in a machine and also comes in a range of weights.

Stretch cotton

Usually a blend of predominantly cotton with a small percentage of elastane, stretch cotton is a great material to use for dress-making, though it's perhaps not well-suited to quilting. With its stretch properties, it's not the most practical to sew.

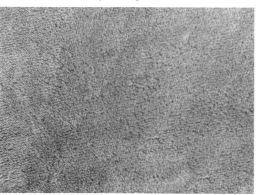

Fleece

Fluffy and fuzzy, fleecing is an incredibly warm and comforting knit fabric that would work perfectly on functional quilts. Bear in mind that fleece has a little bit of stretch to it, so be sure not to pull at it too much when working with it.

Corduroy

A fun and retro choice, corduroy is a thick woven fabric with distinct ridges (known as wales). It's an easy fabric type to work with and is also extremely durable, and its texture contrasts nicely with plain cotton or silk.

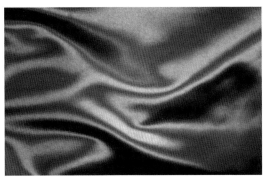

Velvet
When working with velvet you must be extra careful with the nap of the fabric. Using a fine needle, always sew in the direction of the nap.

Silk
Extremely lightweight and delicate, silk has a premium look and feel, but the cost is that it's tricky to work with. Edges fray very easily, so you need to be extra careful when finishing the fabric, and silk can only be dry-cleaned.

Denim
Denim is a hardwaring fabric that is very versatile in its uses, and you can easily reuse old jeans and denim jackets for your projects. Use a special denim needle and walking foot. New denim should always been pre-washed as the dye is prone to running.

Linen
Linen is a breathable material made from the flax plant. You can get hold of it in many weights and colours, but it can be expensive and difficult to work with. Zigzag stitch to minimise fraying while working with it.

Wool
Like cotton, this natural material is a popular choice, though its delicate nature makes it somewhat trickier to work with. Wool can usually only be dry-cleaned.

A guide to the lingo
When it comes to buying fabric there are plenty of terms that are thrown around, and for any casual observer it can seem like an entirely new language. So what exactly does it mean when you hear about the selvedge, the bias and the grain?

First of all, selvedge is what seamstresses mean when they refer to the finished edges off the bolt of fabric. This is usually where you'll see a border with writing, company details and colour swatches on the end. If someone talks about cutting on the bias, they mean that the fabric has been cut into at a 45-degree angle from the selvedge. Cutting on the bias is a popular method, as it actually has a little bit of stretch to it and the fabric tends to fray slightly less. Finally, the grain simply refers to how the material is woven together. Those are just the basics, but you are sure to pick up on the lingo as you go along.

Precut fabrics

For the ultimate precision for beginners, pick up a precut fabric to build your quilt

Cutting your own fabric is one thing, but as a beginner (and even as an expert) it can be much easier to use precut materials. Craft shops will often have a good selection of fat quarters, charms and rolls for you to buy. Most fabric shops will also sell them made up of old scraps, or offcuts from the bolts. And even if you don't need them, adding to your stash is always recommended!

Fat quarter

The most popular type of precut fabric, a fat quarter measures 18x22in (46x56cm). They're particularly useful if you're working with patterned material, as there's a larger pattern repeat.

Fat eighths

Half the size of a fat quarter, a fat eighth measures approximately 9x22in (23x56cm).

Strip/Jelly Roll

These rolls feature strips of fabric that measure 2.5x44in (6.5x112cm), going from one end of the material's selvedge to the other. Usually you'll find about 40 strips of fabric in a roll, though this will depend on the manufacturer.

Diecuts

These cuts are fairly unique, as they are precut pieces of material that come in particular shapes. They're particularly handy if you want to decorate your quilt with some appliqué.

Layer Cakes

Featuring a collection of complementary fabrics and prints, a Layer Cake provides around 42 pieces of 10x10in (25.5x25.5cm) precut pieces of fabric.

Charm Packs

Similar to the Layer Cake but smaller, a Charm Pack features 5x5in (12.5x12.5cm) squares of material. Charm Packs are usually available in sets of 40, though you can get smaller packs if you need them.

Wadding

Give your quilts substance and structure with any of these kinds of filling

For most quilting projects you will need to layer up your fabrics with a middle section of wadding. These come in a variety of types that provide different finishes and weights. Thicker waddings will create warmer duvets whereas finer fillings will provide you with a thinner blanket. The choice is really up to you, so let us take you through the different types.

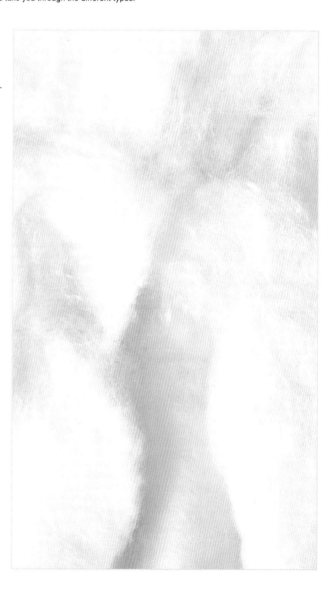

Cotton
Cotton filling provides a relatively lightweight filling that's thin, soft and natural. It's cheap, though it's not particularly insulating and doesn't provide much warmth.

Polyester
Lightweight and inexpensive, polyester wadding is great for tighter budgets. As it's synthetic, you'll find that it's quite warm, though it's non-breathable so shouldn't be used for baby blankets.

Cotton-polyester blend
Combining the best of both cotton and polyester, a blend provides warmth in a lightweight wadding, while offering a little more texture and bounce.

Toy stuffing
For any three-dimensional elements on your quilt, toy stuffing (usually made of polyester, but occasionally wool or cotton) is ideal. It's generally inexpensive and enables you to be more creative with your projects.

Bamboo
Soft but durable, bamboo wadding is very breathable and can be easily worked on a machine. It's also very lightweight, so you'll find that it drapes elegantly.

Wool
A favourite for providing the ultimate warmth and weightlessness, the drawback of using wool wadding is that it's the most expensive option on this list.

TOP TIP When buying wadding, take the final intended size of your quilt top and add an extra 6in (15cm) to its width and length.

Preparing fabric

These are some important steps you need to take before starting a quilting project

Before you start any project you will need to prepare your fabric. This not only makes sure that you have the correct amounts for your chosen pattern, but it also ensures that the fabric is clear of blemishes and ready for your needs. Pre-washing your fabric is key for any project as the fibres may shrink and move, which you won't want to happen after you start.

Pre-washing and pre-shrinking

So your fabric's chosen and you're one step closer to creating your dream quilt — but don't be too hasty and skip the preparation step. It's important to give your fabric a wash before you make any adjustments to the material. There are a few important reasons for this — first of all, you want to wash out any excess dye from the material, as any residue could transfer to another patch of colour through rubbing or if the quilt is washed later down the line. Secondly, it'll get rid of any unwanted chemicals lurking in the weave of your fabric. Washing it will also rid the material of any unwanted creases, so you'll have quite literally a blank canvas for your work.

Most importantly, however, pre-washing your material relaxes and shrinks the fabric — known as pre-shrinking. Most materials shrink in their first wash, so by pre-shrinking your material you'll have a more accurate idea of what you'll be working with, and you'll be able to control it much more easily.

When washing material, be sure to check fabric washing details and ensure that similarly coloured fabrics are washed together. Keep the wash cool and use a mild detergent (or even baby shampoo). Once washed, lay your fabric on a counter and wipe out any creases. You'll want to iron your material before you make any cuts or stitches.

Cutting your fabric

You've probably heard quilters talk about fat quarters. A fat quarter is a certain cut of fabric that measures 18x22in (23x56cm).. To create one, cut half a yard of fabric to get a piece that measures 18x44in (23x112cm). Next, you'll cut it into half again. If you're unsure about cutting fabric, packs of fat quarters can be picked up at shops.

To wash or not to wash?

Many quilters debate whether you really need to wash your fabrics before you start quilting. Some situations are certain — if you're making a quilt that will be used by babies or those with sensitive skin, or if you're planning for it to be regularly used in the house, then you'll want to wash it to get rid of any irritants, chemicals or loose dye.

However, there are several reasons why you might want to save the wash until the end. Purely ornamental quilts might benefit from not being washed as the colours remain bold and as vibrant as the materials were when they were first bought. If you've picked up a precut quilting kit, you should save the wash until the end — as you'll likely lose one of the small pieces in the washing machine, or they might shrink unevenly.

From a purely aesthetic point of view, washing the quilt once it's complete can give you a rustic, antique look that many quilters aspire towards. The choice is yours!

Getting started

**Prepare your fabric, create bindings
and the basics of building**

*"When cutting any shape,
remember to account for seam
allowances"*

Anatomy of a quilt

So now you've got your sewing basics and your fabric, it's time to look at what makes a quilt

A quilt is made up of three basic layers — the quilt top, wadding and the backing — which together are known as the quilt sandwich. However, there are five main elements you need to actually put together your quilt. The first is a finished quilt top, which will most often be a patchwork design you've already sewn together. This can be made up of a repeating block pattern or a mismatched design, and could include sashing and borders.

The second element is the wadding, which gives the quilt its weight and warmth. Make sure to give the type of wadding you use some consideration, taking into account who the quilt is for and when it is most likely to be used.

After the wadding, you'll add your backing as the third element. This can be a patchwork design like the quilt top if you so choose, or just a simple piece of plain or patterned fabric.

The fourth element is quilting, which serves two functions as part of your quilt. First, it holds all three parts of the quilt sandwich together to ensure a high-quality finished product. Second, it adds texture to the quilt — the more quilting you add, the more rigid the quilt will become. Again, consider the uses of the quilt when deciding how much or little to do.

The final element to add to the quilt is the binding — a strip of fabric sewn around the edge to seal the raw edges. This will give your quilt a professional look and ensure the edges don't get tatty over time.

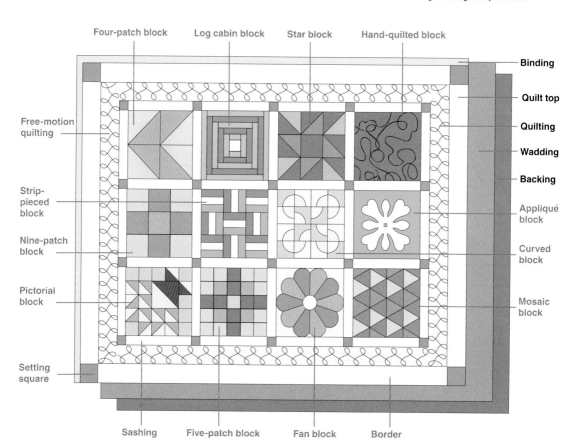

Four-patch block   Log cabin block   Star block   Hand-quilted block

Binding

Quilt top

Quilting

Wadding

Backing

Free-motion quilting

Strip-pieced block

Nine-patch block

Pictorial block

Setting square

Appliqué block

Curved block

Mosaic block

Sashing   Five-patch block   Fan block   Border

Quilting measurements

Choosing what size to make your quilt can be daunting

You can make quilts in a variety of sizes — from very small ones for newborns to enormous ones to cover a superking-size bed, and everything in between. And while there's no problem with just making one as big or small as you like, sometimes you'll want the perfect fit. For that, you'll need to know the exact measurements you're aiming for, before you even begin gathering your materials. The best way to get the perfect fit for your quilt is to measure where you want it to cover. However, this may not always be possible — for example, if the quilt you're making is going to be a surprise gift for someone. If that's the case, use standard measurements for the nearest possible size for the fit you want. If the quilt is for yourself, or for somewhere that you have easy access to in order to take measurements, use this guide to get a quilt that'll fit precisely where you want it to.

Assess the size

01 Measure the bed

With a tape measure (and maybe someone to help you), accurately measure and record the size of the bed that you want the quilt to cover. You will need to gather the measurements of the length, width and depth of the bed.

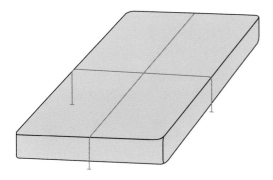

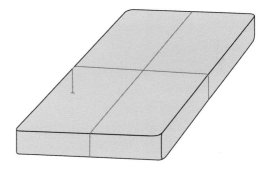

02 Using the depth measurement

To ensure the quilt covers the three exposed sides of the bed, you will need to add the depth measurement to the width twice (to allow for both lengthways sides), and once to the length measurement (to cover the bottom). Now you have the measurements to make a quilt that will precisely cover your bed.

03 Calculate a drop

You may want the quilt to hang a bit past the measurements of the bed. In this case, choose how much you w ould like the quilt to drop by (usually an inch/a few centimetres) and add this measurement twice to the width measurement and once to the length measurement.

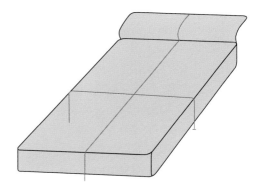

Standard quilt sizes	
Baby	30in x 40in
Crib	36in x 52in
Throw	50in x 65in
Twin	70in x 90in
Double	85in x 108in
Queen	90in x 108in
King	110in x 108in

04 Add a pillow tuck

To make your quilt long enough to also cover the pillows on your bed, you will need to add approximately 18in (45cm). Double check whether this will be enough by measuring the height and depth of the pillows, then add a few extra centimetres for the part that will be tucked underneath.

Cutting fabric

Learn different techniques for cutting your fabrics with a rotary cutter or scissors

Many of today's patterns require you to use a rotary cutter, used in conjunction with your quilter's ruler, it creates more accurate and straighter edges than using scissors. Always use your rotary cutter on a self-healing mat. When cutting any shape, remember to account for seam allowances and always cut away from your body, keeping your fingers away from the blade.

Rotary Cutting

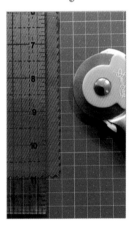

01 Create a straight edge

To begin with, you need to ensure you have a straight edge to your fabric. Fold your fabric to have both selvedges together, place on a mat, align your folded edge with the top and the side of the ruler just inside the selvedge seam, cut steadily along this edge with your rotary cutter (always cut away from your body).

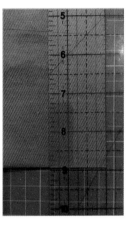

02 Cut the width

Keeping your fabric where it is, turn your mat and place your ruler at the required width of your strip from your cut edge, ensuring your ruler is aligned with both your cut edge and the folded edge to keep it square (use the guidelines on the ruler), cut using the rotary cutter, making sure you cut your strip along the grain of the fabric.

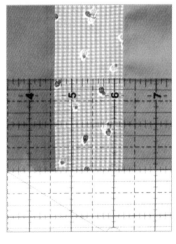

03 Trim into smaller units

Cut a strip into smaller units by placing it on a cutting mat and measuring the required width using your quilter's ruler, cut using a rotary cutter.

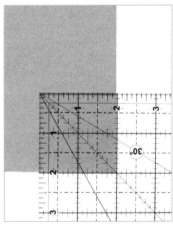

04 Cut shapes

Using the quilter's ruler, you can cut squares and rectangles. Remember to add a seam allowance of ⅞in (2.2cm) when you cut a right-angled triangle and a 1⅜in (2.75cm) if you are cutting quarter-square triangles.

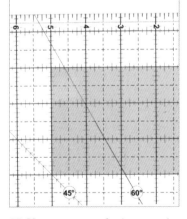

05 Use a pressed piece strip

Work with a pressed pieced strip, straighten the end as necessary. Position your ruler over your pieced strip end that you are going to cut, measure the required width and cut using the rotary cutter.

Cut a pieced strip on the bias

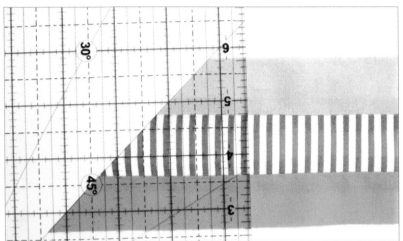

01 Trim at 45-degrees

Trim at a 45-degree angle (using the quilter's ruler) one pieced strip from one end of your pieced strip. Measure against your ruler the required width of strip, keeping the angle the same and cut using a rotary cutter.

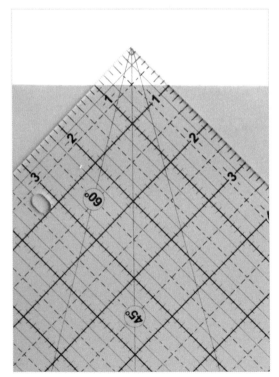

02 Cut the first strip

Straighten the edge of the fabric and cut away the first strip. Using the quilter's ruler, line up the 45-degree mark on the straightened edge and cut the corner piece of fabric away.

03 Cut on the bias

With your quilter's ruler on the cut edge, cut strips to the required width. Cutting fabric on the bias causes it to stretch, so care should be taken in both cutting and sewing.

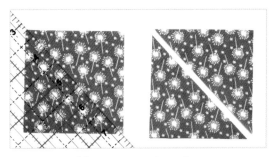

Create half-square triangles

Cut your square of material large enough to include a seam allowance, then using a rotary cutter, cut half-square triangles by cutting across the diagonal of the square.

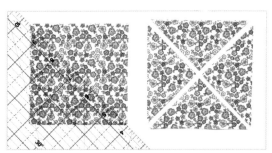

Cut quarter-square triangles

Cut your square of material large enough to include the seam allowance. Using a rotary cutter, cut diagonally from each corner to form four quarter-square triangles.

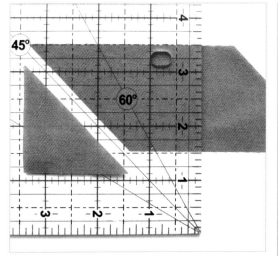

Make 45-degree diamonds or triangles

Cut a length of material wide enough for your diamond and including seam allowance. Using your quilter's ruler, cut a 45 degree angle from one end, then aligning your ruler along the cut edge make a second cut to the width of your diamond.

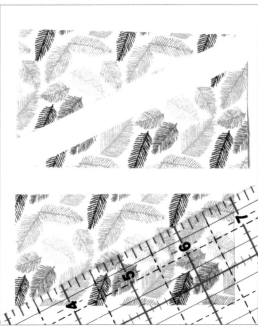

Cut irregular triangles

Cut a rectangle of material large enough to include your seam allowance. As with the square, cut across the diagonal to form two irregular triangles. To make matching irregular triangles, cut a second rectangle of material, but cut across the opposite corners.

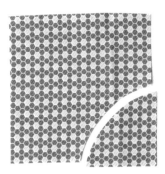

Cut curves

Measure down two sides of your square (this ensures the curve cut will be even). Mark your curve onto the wrong side of your material and cut with a rotary cutter. If the curve is quite small, it may be better to use a small blade instead.

TOP TIP

Purchase a cutting mat marked in inches as mats with other craft marks on them could cause confusion while cutting.

Cut by hand

Rotary cutters are great for cutting large pieces of fabric, but most quiltmakers swear by scissors when it comes to cutting out smaller or more intricate shapes. It's usually a good idea to have at least two sets of scissors on hand, with one for fabric and others for paper, template plastic, wadding and the like, as using fabric scissors on materials other than fabric can quickly blunt the blades.

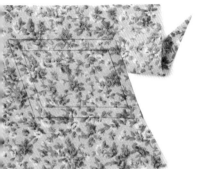 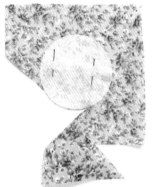 

Cut without a pattern

Start by drawing the outline of the your shape on the wrong side of the fabric. Be sure to measure carefully and add a seam allowance if needed. Cut around the shape using fabric scissors, or cut a short distance from it if you haven't marked out a line for the seam allowance.

Cut with a pattern

Draw your shape straight onto a piece of paper or tracing paper to make a template, pin it to the fabric and use scissors to cut around it. Using a pattern means you can reuse it to cut out several pieces of fabric of the same size and shape.

Fussy cutting

This method is used to isolate a specific feature on the fabric, like a motif on patterned fabric or appliqué, by cutting out a window to view it through. Fussy cutting can sometimes seem overly complicated and a waste of fabric, but its effect is usually worth the hassle.

Unpick a seam

When dealing with fabric and thread, it's pretty easy to make the occasional mistake. Even experienced quiltmarkers sometimes find themselves needing to go back and unpick. Some patterns even require it during construction. In these instances, put away the scissors and use a seam ripper.

Method 1

Start by drawing the outline of the your shape on the wrong side of the fabric. Be sure to measure carefully and add a seam allowance if needed. Gently pull the layers of fabric apart as you work to the end of the seam.

Method 2

Before pressing the seam, hold it taut and use the seam ripper to break the thread every third or fourth stitch along. Gently pull the pieces of fabric apart to separate them and open the seam. Do not use this method on bias seams.

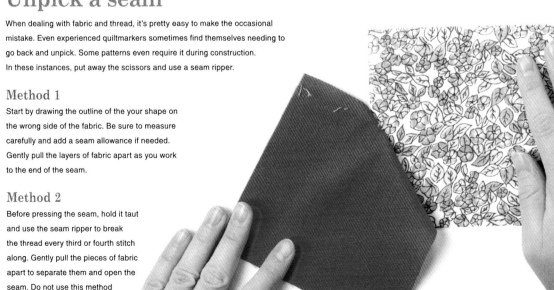

Hand stitches

Discover how to start and end your projects with our simple tips

Like with all crafts, there are several ways you can start and end your projects. It comes down to what you prefer to do, what works best for you, or what works best for the project. Here we'll show you techniques for your first stitches, and the best ways to tie off at the very end. You might find there is another method that works even better, but this is a good place to start!

Backstitched loop

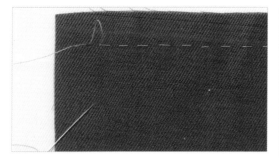

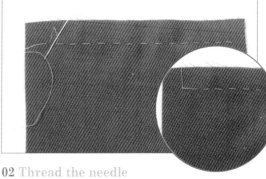

01 Leave a loop
This method is a secure way to finish a line of stitching, even though it doesn't have the bulk of a knot. Backstitch once at the end of a line, leaving a loop, but being careful not the pull the thread taut.

02 Thread the needle
Take the needle through the loop and pull the thread tight to finish the line and secure the thread.

Double backstitched loop

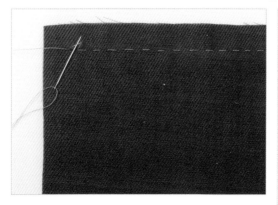

01 Create a second loop
If you're not convinced by the backstitch loop, this method is even more secure. Backstitch once at the end of a line, leaving a small loop as in Step 1 (above). Push the tip of the needle through the loop to form a second loop, creating a figure of eight.

02 Insert the needle
Insert the tip of the needle in the new loop.

03 Pull tight
Pull the thread taut to form a secure knot.

Hand stitches for quiltmaking

Most quilts today are made with the help of an electric sewing machine, but sometimes you will be required to go back to the basics of a needle, thread and old-fashioned elbow grease. There are a number of techniques that require hand sewing, and it's important to select the correct stitch for the best result.

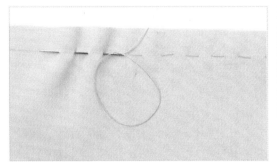

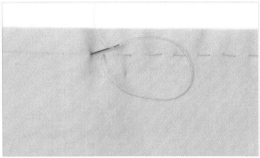

Running stitch

This is the most common stitch for hand sewing. Start by taking the needle in and out of the fabric several times where you want the stitch to appear, making small, evenly spaced stitches. Pull the needle through until the thread is taut, and repeat until the end of the seam.

Stab stitch

Sometimes it's not possible to complete a running stitch, like if you are trying to sew through several layers or into thick fabric. In these instances, a stab stitch is a good alternative. Take the needle through the fabric vertically from the top and pull until the thread is taut. For the next stitch, take the needle through vertically from below. Repeat until you have reached the end of the seam.

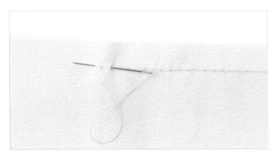

Backstitch

Backstitch can be used as another alternative to a running stitch, creating a continuous line. Start by bringing the needle through the layers of fabric on the right side before inserting it a short distance behind where it emerged. Bring it back to the right side the same distance in front of where it first emerged, and repeat until the end of the seam.

Oversewing

Also known as whipstitch or overcasting, oversewing is used to join two edges to create an almost invisible seam. Tac the layers of fabric in place, and bring the needle through the back edge to the front edge, picking up a few threads from each edge as you go. Gently pull the thread until it is taut, but not tense, and repeat to the end of the seam.

Slip stitch

This method is used mainly in appliqué and to seam together edges that can't be reached with a sewing machine. It joins two pieces of fabric together with an almost invisible line of stitching. Start by knotting the thread and bringing the needle to the front, hiding the knot within the folded edge of the top piece, before taking the needle vertically through the folded edge of the bottom piece. Move the thread along inside the bottom piece's fold and pull the thread through to create a stitch. Take the thread through the folded edge of the top piece from the top, and continue to the end of the seam.

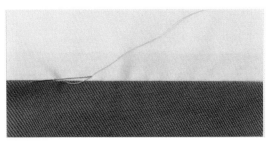

Pressing

Ensure your patchwork is accurate by pressing with an iron

I t may not be one of the more enjoyable aspects of patchworking, but pressing is essential when it comes to making sure the patchwork is accurate and lines up correctly. Pressing is different to ironing, which can often cause fabric and seams to distort. When pressing, use the iron to press down in one place on the seam before lifting it and pressing down in a different area. It's important to remember to press seams towards the darker fabric to prevent darker colours from showing through lighter fabrics, and to make sure the temperature of the iron is appropriate to the fabric you are pressing. Here we will show you the best techniques.

Press seams

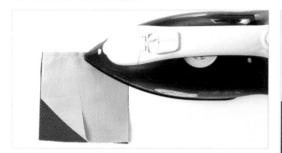

01 Press straight seams

Place the sewn strips on the ironing board with the right sides together and the darker fabric on top. Carefully press the iron along the seam, lifting it at regular intervals so as not to burn the fabric. This is called 'setting the seam', and helps to ensure the accuracy by locking the threads in place and smoothing the fibres of the fabric.

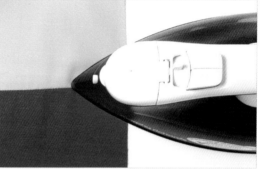

02 Open and press again

Open the sewn strips to the right sides and use the iron to press from one end to the other along the seam until it is flat and even.

Work in rows

When working in rows, minimise bulkiness where the seams join by pressing the seams of adjoining rows in opposite directions from one another.

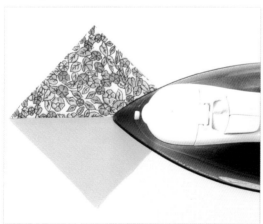

03 Press bias seams

Lift and replace the iron while working along the straight grain to prevent the seam from accidentally being pulled out of shape.

Press a pieced block

Place the block the wrong side up on the ironing board and use the iron to carefully press the seams, making sure they lie as flat as possible.

Press seams open

Where several seams meet, it is possible to reduce the bulk of the fabric by pressing the seams open. After setting the seam, turn the piece to the wrong side, open the seam and press along the length of it with the tip of the iron.

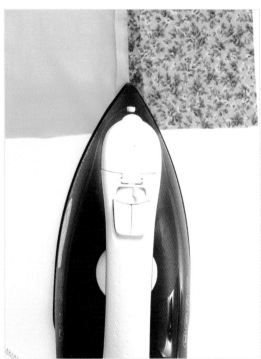

Alternative methods

Thumbnail

It is not always necessary to use an iron when pressing seams. While working on a hard surface, open the fabric strips and run your thumbnail gently along the seam line, first on the wrong side and then the right, pressing the lighter fabric towards the darker one.

Small wooden iron

Working on the wrong side of the fabric, place the flat, chisel-shaped edge of the tool on the seam line and run it gently along the seam.

Hera

A hera marker is a small plastic hand tool with a sharp edge, designed to leave a temporary crease when dragged across the surface of a piece of fabric.

Assembling a quilt

Now it's time to make your quilt sandwich and bring it all together

After marking out the quilt pattern on the quilt top, assembling the quilt 'sandwich' is the next step. The sandwich is formed from the layers of top fabric, wadding and backing fabric that make up the quilt. If the wadding has been folded, open it, lay it flat and leave it for several hours to relax the wrinkles. Here we show you a couple of different methods.

01 Trim and secure

Trim the wadding and backing around 3-6 in (7.5-15cm) larger all around than the finished top layer. Lay the backing the wrong side up on a work surface, smooth it flat, and secure it to the surface with pieces of masking tape.

02 Centre the wadding

Centre the wadding onto the backing, and smooth it out.

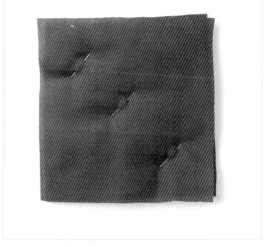

03 Add the top layer

Centre the top layer of the quilt on to of the wadding, positioning it with the right side facing upwards. Use a ruler to ensure to top is squared up. Temporarily pin along each squared up edge as you work.

04 Pin the layers together

Tack or pin the layers together, being sure to work from the centre out diagonally, horizontally and vertically. Remove the pins along the edge as you reach them, and carefully smooth the layers. If tacking, take stitches 2in (5cm) long. If pinning, use safety pins and follow the same pattern while inserting the pins at 3-4in (7.5-10cm) intervals.

Make a bigger backing

As most bed quilts are wider than most fabrics, it's often necessary to piece the backing. There are several ways to do this, but you should always avoid having the seam down the vertical centre of the quilt.

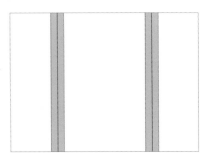

01 Cut the fabric

Start by cutting two full widths of fabric of the required length for your quilt. Cut one piece in half lengthways and trim off all selvedges.

02 Join them

Add one half-width to either side of the full piece of fabric to get the required width.

Bagging out

Sometimes it's best to finish the edges of the quilt before you quilt it, especially while working on smaller projects like baby quilts. To do this, you will need to cut the wadding and backing slightly larger than the quilt top.

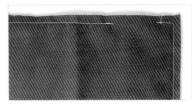

01 Arrange the layers

Centre the quilt top right side up on the wadding, and centre the backing on top of that right side down. Keep the layers in place by pinning or tacking them together around the edge.

02 Stitch together

Machine stitch the layers from the bottom edge, several centimetres from the corner, taking in a ¼in (6mm) seam and secure with a few backstitches.

03 Leave an opening

Stop ¼in (6mm) from the edge with the needle down when you reach the corners. Raise the presser foot, pivot the fabric 90-degrees and continue sewing the seam. On the final side, leave an opening of 5-10in (12-25cm) and secure with backstitches.

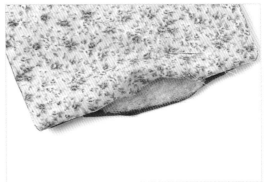

04 Cut the excess

Clip off the corners to reduce bulk, and trim and grade the seams if needed. Turn the right side out through the opening on the final side.

05 Blind stitch the square

Level the edges on the inside before pinning and pressing lightly. Blind stitch the opening closed to complete the quilt.

Binding

Learn how to make binding strips and calculate meterage

P re-made bias binding is available to buy in a variety of colours and widths, but sometimes it's better to make your own. Bindings should be applied as a continuous strip; if possible, cut straight binding strips along the lengthways grain of the fabric or join pieces before applying. Bias binding is suitable for binding work with curved edges as it has a bit more stretch than straight binding.

Make a straight binding strip

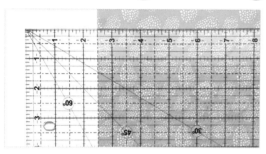

01 Measure and cut

Measure the edges of the piece being bound and choose a width for the binding strip. Cut out strips six times the chosen width, adding an extra ¼in (6mm) for extra length for mitring corners and joining pieces.

02 Cut along the straight grain

Make sure the edges of the fabric pieces are square, and cut along the straight grain. Add about 16in (40cm) extra to the length for full-sized quilts, 12in (30cm) for baby quilts, large embroideries and wall hangings, and 8in (20cm) for small pieces.

Make a bias strip

01 Remove selvedges

Starting with at least 59in (150cm) of fabric, cut off selvedges and smooth the fabric flat. Straighten the right-hand edge, and then fold the edge back so that it aligns with the top edge and forms an exact 45-degree angle. Cut along the bias fold.

02 Mark out lines

Using a ruler and a sharp piece of tailor's chalk, mark out lines parallel to the bias edge. Cut out the strips, plus as many as you need for your project and a few extra, just in case.

03 Join the strips

Join the strips together to create one long, continuous strip. Pin them together at a 90-degree angle with right sides facing and sew a ¼in (6mm) seam on the bias. The seam should end up running from edge to edge of each strip, with a triangle of fabric left at either end of the seam.

04 Press the seam

Use an iron to press the seam open before trimming off the seam allowances and the extending triangles on the edges. The prepared strips can also be used to make bias binding by pressing the edges or running the strip through a bias binding maker.

Make a continuous bias strip

01 Cut two triangles from a square

Cut out a square of binding fabric with 90-degree corners, marking two opposite sides as A and B and drawing a diagonal line from corner to corner. Cut along the line.

02 Join them together

Take the two resulting triangles and place the right sides together. Join the pieces where they overlap using a tight stitch length. Press the seam open and trim the dog ears.

03 Mark lines

Mark lines parallel to the bias edge to your chosen width.

04 Make a tube

Bring the last two straight-grain edges together and offset the marked lines by aligning the lines as you fold the fabric in on itself. Pin to match the marked lines and sew together, right sides facing, to make a tube.

Calculating meterage

To calculate how much binding will come from one piece of fabric, multiply the length of the fabric by the width, then divide by the width of the cut binding strip. For example, for a 2in (5cm) wide binding strip cut from a 36in (90cm) square of fabric you will get 36x36in = 1,296in (90x90cm = 8,100cm). Divide by 2in (5cm) to get 648in (1,620cm). You can make 18yd (16.2m) of binding, which should be enough for a king-sized quilt. Remember to always work in either the metric or the imperial systems when doing your calculations.

05 Make a continuous strip

Cut along your now aligned marked lines to make one continuous strip that you can use.

Bind with pre-made bias binding

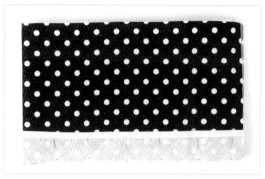

01 Pin the tape

After squaring the quilt, measure all four sides, add them together, then add approximately 16in (40cm) to the total length. Open the folded edges of the bias tape, and align along one side of the quilt top, make sure you start in the middle of the side, with the side of the bias tape pictured facing up. Pin to secure.

02 Stitch the tape

Machine stitch along the outside edge of the tape through all the layers, beginning a few centimetres from the end of it. Use a seam allowance a quarter the width of the bias tape, with the stitch landing approximately on the fold.

04 Remove from the presser foot

Pull the quilt out from under the presser foot, but do not cut the threads or pull them out too far.

03 Leave a seam allowance

At the end of the edge, stop stitching a seam allowance's distance from the corner and back stitch a few stitches.

05 Make a mitred corner

Create a mitred corner by folding the tape at a 45-degree angle to the right of the quilt top, with the tape running parallel with the bottom edge of the quilt.

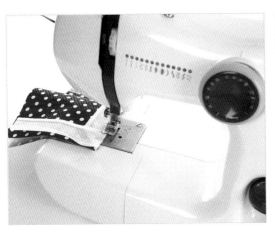

06 Fold it back and pin

Fold the binding back over on itself 180-degrees to the left, with the edge still running parallel with the quilt's edge, and pin in place.

08 Trim and connect

Repeat Steps 2-7 until you are approximately 12in (30cm) from the starting point. Measure the distance between the finishing point and the starting end of the binding tape. Trim the last end and connect the two ends of the tape so that they fit along the final edge of the quilt, then finish stitching the binding in place.

07 Continue stitching

Turn the quilt 90-degrees and put it back under the presser foot, being sure to insert the needle back into the quilt in the same place you finished sewing in Step 3. Continue stitching down the next side.

09 Fold it back

Fold the binding to the back of the quilt, neatly mitring each corner as you go along. Fold the long raw edge of the binding tape that had been open and pin in place.

10 Slip stitch the binding

Using a needle and thread, carefully slip stitch the binding to the back side of the quilt, enclosing the raw edges and covering stitches made from machine sewing the binding to the front. Secure and embed the knot inside the quilt when you finish.

Turned-edge binding

Adding a turned edge binding is another simple way of finishing off the edge of a quilt, but this method doesn't require a binding strip. Instead, the binding is formed by folding the backing of the quilt to the front and stitching it in place, giving it the appearance of traditional bias binding.

01 Pin and trim

Pin back the backing fabric and trim the wadding and the quilt top so that they are the same size. Unpin the backing fabric, and trim it to twice the width you want the turned-edge binding to be once it is complete.

02 Pin a corner

Fold one corner of the backing fabric over the cover of the top of the quilt and pin it in place. Trim off the tip of the backing fabric.

03 Fold the edge

Fold the edge next to the backing fabric so that it aligns with the edges of the wadding and quilt top.

04 Fold again and pin

Fold the edge of the backing fabric over a second time so that it overlaps with the quilt top and creates an edge the desired width of your binding. Pin the folded edge in place.

05 Repeat and trim if needed

Repeat Steps 2-4 for each edge and corner, making sure edges meet in neat mitres at the corners. If there are any trimmed corners from Step 2 visible, trim them until they are matching.

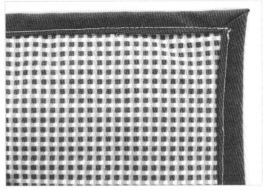

06 Slip stitch or machine stitch

Use a slip stitch on the turned-edge binding to attach it to the top of the quilt. Alternatively, you can machine stitch along each edge.

Double-fold binding

For projects that will get a lot of wear, like bed quilts, a double-fold binding is useful as it is stronger than bias tape binding.

01 Cut strips of binding fabric

Cut out strips of binding fabric six times the width of your finished binding, plus ¼in (6mm) extra. Cut enough strips to run around your quilt top, about 16in (40cm) extra. Join them all together, fold the strip in half lengthways, wrong sides together, and press.

02 Pin the strips

Lay the binding strip along an edge on the right side of the quilt, with the unworked edges together. Pin the strip in place along the first side, starting about half way along and making sure none of the joined binding seams land on a corner.

03 Machine stitch

Begin machine stitching about 8in (20cm) from the start of the binding using the seam allowance of the desired width of the binding. Mitre the binding whenever you meet a corner, and keep working down the edges. Pin it in place and continue to sew the next side until all of the sides have binding attached. Join the ends.

04 Slip stitch to finish

Turn the folded edge to the back of the quilt and mitre the corners. Slip stitch the binding in place.

Patchwork

**Learn the techniques you need
for the basics of patchwork**

> *"Piecing can be worked by hand or machine, though machining will be much quicker"*

Hand piecing

Sew two bits of fabric together with the help of some essential piecing techniques

Piecing is the art of sewing together pieces of fabric. These can be single pieces or pieced units made into a large patchwork design, starting with two small pieces of fabric and joining with others to create a larger piece of work. Piecing can be worked by hand or machine, though machining will be much quicker. Although it is easier to sew with squares or rectangles, you can piece with any shape, like triangles, curves, diamonds, and so on.

It is important to mark your seam allowance on both pieces, on the wrong side of the fabric units to ensure an accurate sewing line. Bias-cut or shaped pieces (especially on curves) can be inclined to stretch on the raw edge, so extra caution is needed when sewing these. You can secure the seam by making a small backstitch whenever you pass the needle through and if on a bias seam, use a double backstitched loop. However, do take care not to sew into your seam allowances.

Hand piecing

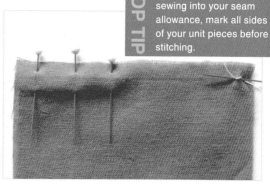

TOP TIP If you are worried about sewing into your seam allowance, mark all sides of your unit pieces before stitching.

01 Joining two units with a straight seam

With your first two units, place the right sides together. You do not sew into the seam allowance on the two outer edges of the fabric, so mark your seam allowance for each side with pins to ensure you do not go over this point when sewing. Place further pins between these two marker pins to hold fabric in place, ensuring the seam allowance guides are matching.

02 Begin to sew

Once it's all pinned and ready to sew, remove your first pin and place your first stitch into the units at that point. You can fasten your thread with either a knot or by making one or two very small backstitches into the seam allowance.

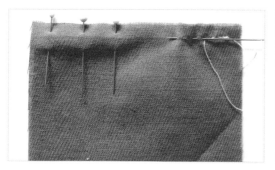

03 Make a running stitch

Run your needle through the fabric to make a few short running stitches along the seamline all at once, pull through the thread, continue along the seamline (remove pins as you go) until you reach the seam allowance at the end.

04 Check the stitching

Regularly check the reverse of your work to ensure the stitching is on the seamline. Stop sewing when you reach the pin and secure the thread the end by working a couple of backstitches.

Joining hand-pieced rows

In the same way as joining two units where you do not sew across the seam allowance, it is again necessary to avoid this when joining together hand-pieced row units.

01 Press the seams and pin

Having sewn your hand-piece, press your seams towards the solid colour. With right sides together line up your two hand-pieced units, matching all sewn seam lines on both sides and pin together. Pin at your matching seams, through all layers as well as at intervals along the row and at either end to hold your work in place.

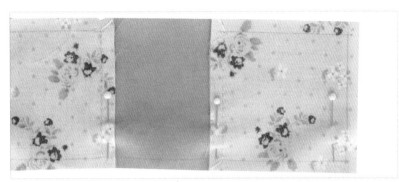

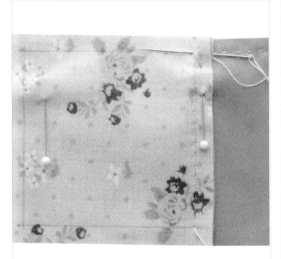

02 Begin sewing

Begin sewing at one end of your work, as before when working in straight seams, make one or two small backstitches at the start of your work or knot your thread. Sew your running stitch along your seam line until you come to the first seam intersection. Instead of sewing across your seam allowances, sew through the seam intersection as shown in picture. To make it more secure, sew an extra backstitch into these intersections as you go.

03 Continue sewing and backstitch

Continue to sew along your hand-pieced unit in this manner until you come to the end of your row. Finish with a backstitched loop (see page 36).

04 Press to finish

To finish, press your new seam to one side, to the one with more dark units if possible.

Machine piecing

Piece several pieces of fabric together using a machine

Machine piecing is a fast way of creating a 'piece' by sewing several pieces of fabric together.

As always, ensure that you have the right-sides together with matching raw edges whilst ensuring you include your seam allowance for each piece of fabric. Seam allowances will be 6mm or ¼ inch unless specified otherwise.

This final piece can be used as a whole or cut into several strips and used in a larger project.

Joining two or more strips

01 Align edges

Align the raw edges of two strips of fabric with right sides together and pin. Sew along the edge allowing for a ¼in (6mm) seam allowance.

02 Press the seam

Once sewn, press the seam to the darker fabric.

TOP TIP

Make sure you press lighter colours behind dark colours so you can't see the dark colours through the quilt.

03 Sew in the opposite direction

If sewing together several strips, turn your fabric for each additional piece, sewing in the opposite direction prevents your fabric from bowing and ensures your work stays straight. Press all seams in the same direction.

Check seam allowance

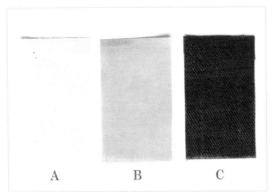

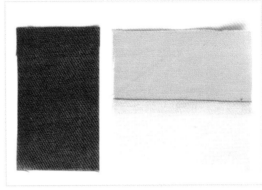

A   B   C

01 Check accuracy

It is important to ensure that when you sew along a seam allowance that it is correct as this will ensure your final work will fit properly. One way to check your machine is doing this correctly is to cut three rectangles all the same size, from three different colour fabrics of 1½x2½in (3.8x6.4cm).

02 Attach Rectangle C

Sew Rectangle A and B together down the long sides using a ¼in (6mm)seam allowance and press the seam to one side. Rectangle C should be the same width as your two joined pieces when laid out. If it is not, you will need to adjust the position of your needle and re-work until it is correct.

Chain piecing

01 Piece paired units together

Pin (right sides together) several paired units ready to be machined. Feed each unit through the machine one after another sewing along the seam allowance line, do not lift the presser foot or break the thread as you go, continue until all are sewn. This will create a chained piece of units held together between short threads.

02 Now separate them

Cut between each unit in the chain.

"It is important to ensure that when you sew along a seam allowance that it is correct"

Intersecting seams

The essential steps for ensuring perfect alignment of patchwork pieces

I t is vital to match the seams perfectly when sewing together patchwork pieces. Doing this ensures that when matching to the next piece, all of the sections perfectly align. You can create precise seams by 'nesting'. This is done by pressing seams in opposing directions, then fitting them into each other. Follow the steps below to help you with this process.

TOP TIP

Pressing your seams after each line is sewn keeps your work flat and even and avoids any puckering.

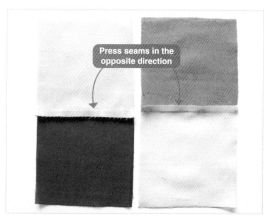

Press seams in the opposite direction

01 Piece and press

Piece together square or rectangle units and press the seams for each joining strip in the opposite direction.

02 Right sides together

Place your joined pieces together, right sides, making sure that you carefully align the seams.

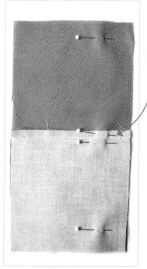

Pin on either side of the seam line

03 Pin

Line up your pieces, nesting the seams and pinning. Feel along the joining seam lines to ensure there is no gap between, and adjust as necessary. The seams should feel smooth once aligned correctly. Pin the pressed seam allowance on both sides of the nested seam. If you have several joins, match all of these first before pinning between.

04 Seam allowance

Sew along the edge using the same seam allowance as on the other pieces. Sew carefully over the matched seams to ensure they stay flat. Press all seams when finished.

Matching seams with points

It is important to match seams accurately when joining up pieces of patchwork. Doing this will give your project the best finish and look. Therefore, matching points on your units is essential.

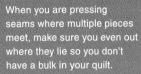

TOP TIP

When you are pressing seams where multiple pieces meet, make sure you even out where they lie so you don't have a bulk in your quilt.

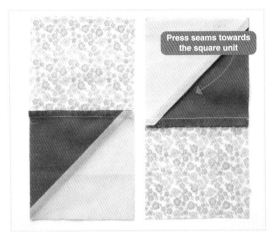

Press seams towards the square unit

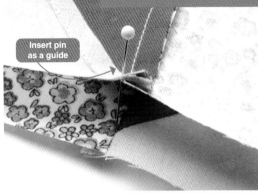

Insert pin as a guide

01 Press them in opposite directions

Press the seams of the pieces to be joined in opposite directions. This allows for less bulk when sewing as well as making it easier to nest the two pieces together.

02 Pin at intersection

With right sides together for your two units, place a pin at the intersecting seam line on the top piece and through to the corresponding point in the bottom piece (as shown above). This will act as your guide for aligning and nesting your pieces.

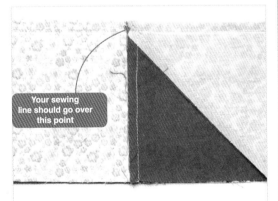

Your sewing line should go over this point

03 Sew together

With your guide pin in place, line up the seam line on your pieces, nesting the seams and pinning. Feel along the joining seam lines to ensure there is no gap between, and adjust as necessary. The seams should feel smooth once aligned correctly. Pin the pressed seam allowance on both sides of the nested seam. If you have several joins, match all of these first before pinning between. Pin along the whole seam, taking into account your seam allowance, and sew.

04 Press and finish

To finish, all that's left to do is to unfold and press all seams. And there you have it!

Set-in seams

Learn the technique for inserting a shape into a set-in corner

P atchwork mainly involves joining pieces of fabric using straight seams, however, occasionally you may need three pieces of fabric where you are inserting a square (or other shape) into a corner. This is known as a set-in seam or a Y-seam. It is important to mark up, and make sure that you are measuring your work carefully. When sewing you must not stitch over the seam allowance and ensure that this is maintained when working into the set-in corner.

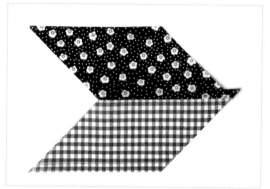

01 Join diamonds

In this example, we are attaching a square into the angle created by joining two diamond-shaped pieces of fabric. Once your diamonds are sewn together, cut a fabric square to fit, marking the ¼ in (6mm) seam allowance along the edges on the wrong side. Mark on this line the start and finish points, being ¼in (6mm) from both edges.

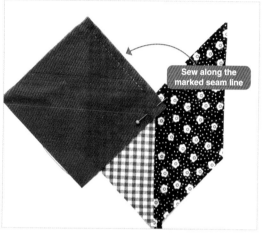

Sew along the marked seam line

02 Right sides together

With right sides together, match the inner point on your square to the seam line of your diamonds (as shown), and continue to pin the two pieces together, matching the edges. Starting from the outer edge, sew along the seam line towards the centre, removing pins as you sew. To secure the corner, make a few small backstitches into the inner corner of the seam, avoiding working into the seam allowance.

Sew along the adjacent seam line

Wrong side

03 Opposite side

Line up your square to the opposite side of the diamond, then pin and sew as in Step 2.

04 Pin

Press your square seam allowance towards the diamonds.

Setting in by machine

Similar to setting the seam by hand, you can also use your machine to achieve the same results, you can create crisp edges in no time at all.

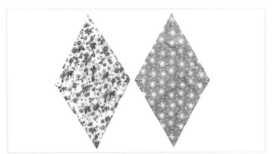

01 Cut your diamonds

Mark a dot ¼in (6mm) in from the side on each corner to be sewn, with a pencil or water-soluble pen. This marks your start and finishing points for sewing and it is important not to sew past these points.

02 Right sides together

Place your two pieces right sides together and pin. Sew between the dots using a ¼in (6mm) seam allowance along one side, making a back stitch at each end. Do not sew past the marked points. Press the seam towards the darker fabric.

03 Dot your work

On your set-in piece, mark a dot at ¼in (6mm) on the wrong side, at the three set-in corners (as shown here).

04 Line up

Line up the next diamond to be set in, right sides together. Match the middle dot with the centre seam dots of the two pieces already sewn together, as well as the outer edge dot on the edges you are joining together. Pin in place and sew from the inner to outer dots, ensuring you do not sew past them.

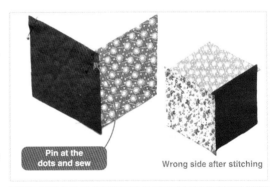

Pin at the dots and sew

Wrong side after stitching

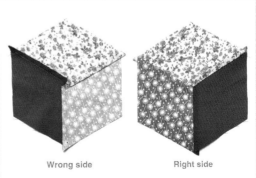

Wrong side

Right side

05 Pin and sew

Match the outer dots on the second side of the piece to be set in as well as the free edge of the unit. Pin together and sew between the inner to outer dots, making a small backstitch at the beginning and end of the sewing line.

06 Press seams

Press all seams flat and in one direction (eg clockwise), snip off corners.

Triangles

Use this versatile method to create an abundance of cool blocks

After squares and rectangles, triangles are one of the most versatile and simplest patchwork shapes to work with. They are a good way to use up small scraps of material and can be used in larger units, borders and many other forms. Further on in the book you will see how you can use triangles to create any number of patterns for use in your quilting projects.

TOP TIP
Mark your seam lines before pinning as this keeps them straight.

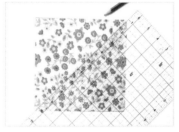

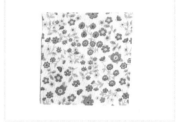

01 Cut your fabric
Cut two squares of contrasting fabric, each of them ⅞in (2.2cm) bigger than you need in the finished piece (this is double the normal seam allowance).

02 Mark your lines
On the wrong side of the fabric, mark a diagonal line in pencil across one square, then pin them together with your second square, with the right sides together.

03 Add extra lines
If easier, pencil in two more lines, ¼in (6mm) along either side of this central line to mark your sewing line, then machine along these lines you have made.

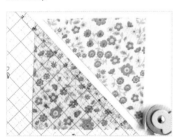

04 Cut fabric
Cut along your marked line with a rotary cutter.

05 Press down
Press your seams open, to create to half-square triangles

Making multiple half-square triangles from strips

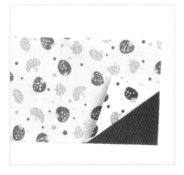

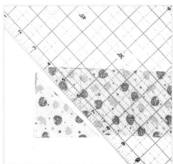

01 Contrasting strips
Cut two strips of contrasting fabric that are ⅞ in (2.2cm) wider than required. On the wrong side of the fabric, mark your squares first, then alternating direction triangles within each square.

02 Mark and cut
As in half-square triangles, pencil two more lines, ¼in (6mm) along either side of this central line to mark your sewing line, then sew along these lines. Using a rotary cutter cut along the marked diagonal and vertical lines to form several half-square triangles. Press your seams.

Making half-square triangles from large pieces

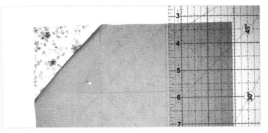
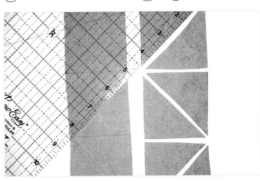

01 Pin your fabric

It is possible to make many half-square triangles from 2 pieces of fabric. Pin 2 pieces of fabric, right sides together and mark using your quilters ruler a grid of squares. Allow for a seam allowance of ⅞in (2.2cm) greater than the finished piece requires.

02 Draw lines

Mark diagonal lines across each of the squares.

03 Sew and press

Sew ¼in (6mm) along both sides of each of these diagonal lines. Using your rotary cutter, cut along the original marked diagonal lines and vertical/horizontal lines to create individual half-square triangles. Press all the seams towards the darker fabric and trim off any excess.

Making a pair of quarter-square triangles

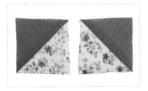

01 Position fabric

Take 2 half-square triangles and then place the right sides together with matching diagonals, while keeping your contrasting fabrics together.

02 Pencil lines

Mark a diagonal line across the pieces in pencil, in the opposite direction, marking across your seam line. Sew ¼in (6mm) along either side of this line.

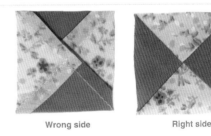

Wrong side   Right side

03 Cut and press

Using your rotary cutter, cut along diagonal line to separate the pieces. Press the seams towards the darker fabric and trim off any excess.

Joining pieced and plain units

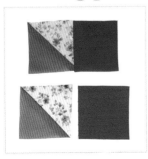

01 Pieced and plain

Place one half-square triangle (the pieced unit) and a plain piece, right sides together. Sew together using a ¼in (6mm) seam allowance. Repeat for the second 2 pieces, ensuring your triangle end points all meet in the centre (layout your pieces before sewing to ensure you have it the correct way).

02 Points in the middle

Line up your pieced units right sides together and sew along the long side. All triangle points should now meet up in the middle of your piece.

Equilateral triangles

01 Cut your fabric

With fabric selected, cut three triangles using your rotary cutter on the 60 degree guide on your quilters ruler.

02 Pin and sew triangles

With right sides together, align and pin two triangles together, marking your seam allowance as necessary and machine sew them, carefully ensuring that you keep the fabric flat and that you are not stretching it as you sew.

03 Press

Open and press the seams towards the darker fabric — this is so it is less visible on the finished item. This also creates 2 small triangles at either end which are known as 'dog ears'.

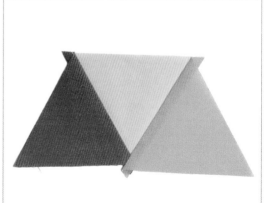

04 Pin and sew

Line up your next triangle using the dog ears as a guide and pin together. Sew along your seam allowance, again, taking care not to stretch the fabric as you sew.

05 Final press

Open and press the seams towards the darker fabric. Repeat the above steps until you have completed your design.

Flying geese

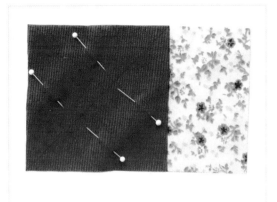

01 Cut your fabric

Cut a rectangle of material that is ¼in (1.2cm) longer and wider than needed for your completed unit. With a contrasting fabric, cut 2 squares that are the same length as the short side of your rectangle. On the wrong side of the fabric, draw a diagonal line between the corners as shown in the picture.

02 Pin and sew squares

With the right sides together, pin your square to align to the left side of the rectangle, but make sure that you position it so that the diagonal is as shown in the picture above. Sew along your seam line slowly and carefully, to ensure that it does not stretch or pucker.

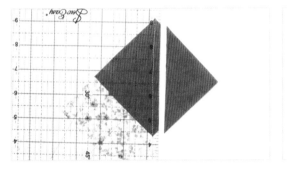

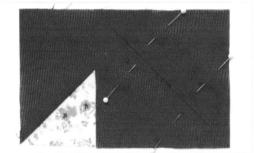

03 Cut the corners

As shown in the picture, align your quilters ruler along your stitched line at the ¼in (6mm) seam allowance. Cut off the corner, trimming the surplus material. Open up your unit and press the seam open.

04 Pin and sew

Follow as in Step 2, however, pin your square to the opposite side of your rectangle with the diagonal placed as shown. Pin your square in place and then sew along the drawn seam line.

05 Press down

As in Step 3, trim off the excess and press your seam open.

TOP TIP

If making several, always start by sewing the square to the same side first, selecting either left or right.

Triangle corners

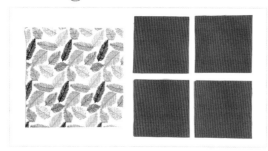

01 Cut your fabric

Cut a square of fabric for your centre piece. Cut 4 more squares in a contrasting fabric, by cutting a square of 2in (5cm) larger than the centre square and cutting it into four equal squares, this will include your seam allowances. Or cut four squares each ¼in (6mm) larger than half the width of your centre square.

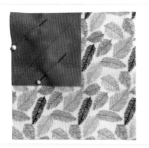

03 Line up and pin squares

Line up your smaller square into the corner of your larger square and pin in place, with diagonal line across as shown.

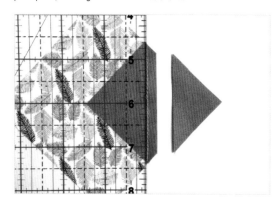

05 Trim the corners

Using your quilters ruler and rotary cutter, trim off the corner leaving a ¼in (6mm) seam allowance).

02 Draw lines

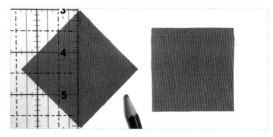

Draw diagonal lines across each of the smaller squares on the wrong side of the material.

04 Sew your lines

Sew through your diagonal line, taking care not to stretch your fabric as you sew.

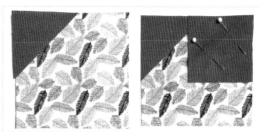

06 Press down

Open up the triangle and press down. Follow the above steps, working clockwise until all four corners are attached.

07 Final press

Press your finished piece.

Sewing triangles to squares

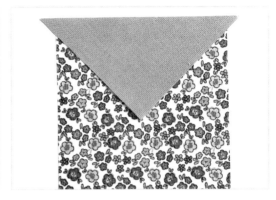

01 Cut your fabric

Cut a square of fabric to your chosen size, then in a contrasting fabric, cut four triangles, their long side should be the same width as the side of your square plus ¼in (6mm) for seam allowance. Mark the centre of the edge of the square on all four sides and on the long edge of the triangles.

02 Position your fabric

Place your fabric, right sides together, matching your centre markings. Your triangle should have its edges overhanging the square by the same amount on both sides if centred correctly.

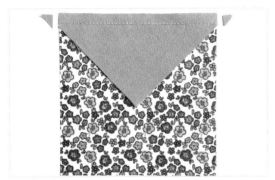

03 Sew and trim

Sew along the seam allowance and trim off the excess small triangles of fabric at either side.

04 Press down

Open up your triangle and press your seam towards the square.

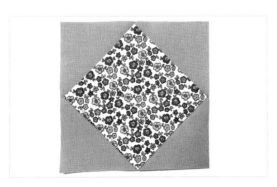

05 Final press

Working clockwise, repeat the above until all triangles are attached to your square, press seams as you work.

TOP TIP

Before you start, see what blocks can be cut next to each other on the fabric, so you don't waste any!

Star blocks

Discover the possible variations of this celestial design

S tar designs make up the largest group of patchwork patterns and add an element of complexity to an otherwise plain quilt. Making star blocks combines many different techniques as they can range from four-patch blocks to elaborate designs with complex layouts. Read on and discover some of the variations you can use in your work.

Single star: Double four-patch

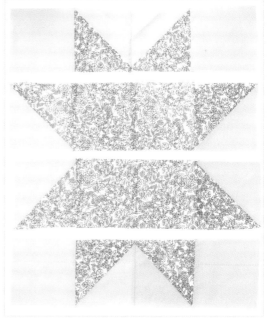

01 Measure and cut

Measure out your squares by dividing the size of the finished block by four, making sure you factor in seam allowances. Cut and make eight half-square triangles from fabrics A and B. Cut an additional four squares each out of fabrics A and B.

02 Assemble in fours

Follow the layout and, with right sides together, stitch the squares and half-square triangles together in rows of four, leaving yourself a 6mm (1/4in) seam allowance.

03 Put it all together

With the right sides together, stitch the rows together while being careful to match the seams and leave a 1/4in (6mm) seam allowance.

Friendship star: Nine-patch

01 Divide by three

Measure out your squares by dividing the size of the finished block by three, making sure you factor in seam allowances. Cut four squares from fabric A and one square from fabric B. Make four half-square triangles from fabrics A and B.

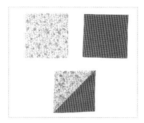

02 Make the rows

Follow the layout and, with right sides together, stitch the squares and half-square triangles together in rows of three, leaving a 1/4in (6mm) seam allowance.

03 Complete the star

With the right sides together, stitch the rows together while being careful to match the seams. Make sure to leave yourself a 1/4in (6mm) seam allowance.

Ohio star: Nine-patch with quarter-square triangles

B

01 Cut the pieces

Measure out your squares by dividing the size of the finished block by three, making sure you factor in seam allowances. Cut four squares from fabric A and one square from fabric B. Cut and make four quarter-square triangles from fabrics A and B.

02 Three groups

Follow the layout and, with right sides together, stitch the squares and quarter-square triangles together in rows of three, leaving a 6mm (1/4in) seam allowance.

03 Bring together

With the right sides together, stitch the rows together while being careful to match the seams and also to leave yourself a 1/4in (6mm) seam allowance.

Hexagon star: 60-degree angles

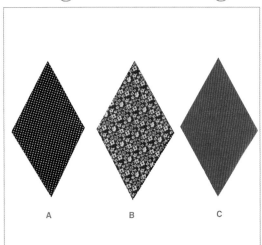

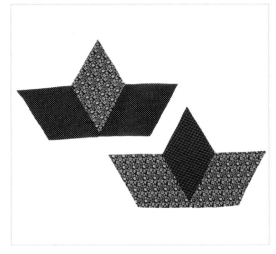

01 Cut some diamonds

Cut 12 60-degree diamonds in three different fabrics, as shown above. Diamonds in fabrics A and B will be the points of the star, while those in fabric C will be the setting diamonds. Add a seam allowance around each when cutting them out.

02 Twist and stitch

With the right sides together and alternating the fabrics, stitch the three star points together in units of three.

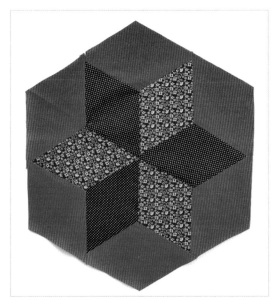

03 Join the halves

Create the star by stitching both units together with the right sides on each touching.

04 Finish up

Complete the block using the setting diamonds.

Eight-point star: 45-degree angles

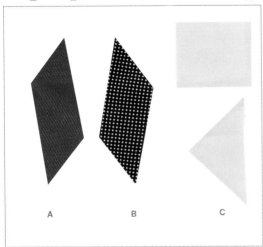

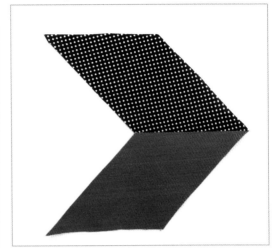

01 Get angular

Make templates to the desired size for the points of the star, the setting triangles and the corner squares. Cut four 45-degree-angle diamonds each from fabrics A and B for the star's points, and four corner squares and four setting triangles from fabric C.

02 Pair up

Stitch the star points in four identical pairs, with the right sides of the fabrics together. Use one fabric A point and one fabric B point to construct each pair.

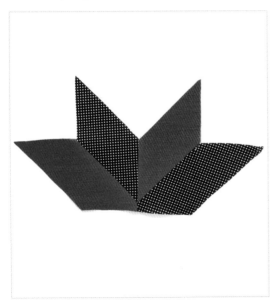

03 Build up the star

Stitch two pairs together, with the right sides together, to make half of the star, and repeat to make the other half. Stitch the two halves together to make a complete star.

04 Set and finish

Set in the setting triangles, and then add the corner squares to complete the block.

Sashing

Show your work off with these sashing techniques

Sashing is the art of framing pieces of fabric and is a really effective way of showing off your block work. It is not necessary to keep your strips the same width — use what looks most effective for your design. The corners of your block can be made more appealing by using setting squares or cornerstones (plain or pieced squares) to your pattern.

Straight-set simple continuous sashing

In this piece each block is framed by straight-set simple sashing.

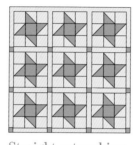

Straight-set sashing with setting squares

Here a square is added between each block, creating an additional pattern. Setting squares can be pieced, pinwheel, four or nine-patch designs.

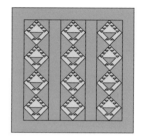

Vertical or horizontal set sashing

Blocks can be constructed in rows with sashing of differing widths between them, running vertically or horizontally.

Diagonal set sashing

Setting blocks on a tilt and assembled in strips can give a chevron effect, extra triangles are added at the edges to join onto the border strips.

Simple continuous sashing

  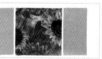

01 Cut the strips

Cut your fabric into sashing strips to your required width plus ½in (1.2cm) seam allowance. All lengths of fabric should be the same as one side of a block.

02 Sew together

With fabric right sides together, sew together a block and strip using a ¼in (6mm) seam allowance; sew alternative blocks and rows until you have completed your row. Press the seams towards the strips.

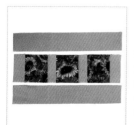

03 Extra sashing

Cut two more strips of sashing to the same length as the finished row. Your width can be the same as your sashing strips or different, but include a seam allowance of ½in (1.2cm).

04 Attach all the pieces

With right sides together, sew your long sashing strips to each side of your pieced row. Press the seams towards the sashing strip. Repeat until all required rows are completed.

Sashing with setting squares

01 Cut strips and squares

Follow Steps 1 and 2 of 'Simple continuous sashing' to create a row of blocks. For the sashing, cut strips of fabric the same length as the width of your block with setting squares the same width as the strips.

02 Alternate pieces

Sew each row of pieces using a ¼in (6mm) seam allowance with right sides together. Follow the pattern shown, alternating squares and strips, creating long sashing strips.

03 Repeat to finish

Place your sashing strips together, right sides, and pin together, taking care to match up all of the seams. Sew the long sashing strips on the bottom and top edges of your centre row of blocks. Follow this method until all rows of blocks and sashing strips are sewn together to create your final quilted piece.

Tilted block setting

 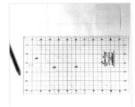  

01 Four pieces

Create your central block, framing it with a wider border made from four pieces of sashing.

02 Create a template

Make a template by marking out the size using tracing paper, including the seam allowance of ½in (1.2cm).

03 Angle as needed

Place the template on top and angle it to the required tilt. Pin in place if necessary by adding one or two pins in the middle of the paper.

04 Mark for later

To be able to keep the same tilt for further blocks, mark in pencil around your centre block onto the tracing paper.

05 Trim excess

Cut off the excess fabric around the template using the rotary cutter and quilters' ruler, make sure the centre block stays in place as you cut.

06 Finish and admire

Your finished block should produce a tilted rotating effect.

Borders

Enhance your quilt with a border that will complement your work

H aving a border on your patchwork can really show off and enhance your finished work. They can be made in several ways using differing widths, single, multiple, pieced or mixed using plain or patterned fabric. Whichever way you do it and whatever fabric you use, it should complement your work. Borders are also important in holding your patchwork edges in place. Border strips should be from one single piece of material and not cut on the bias as this would cause stretch and miss-shaping.

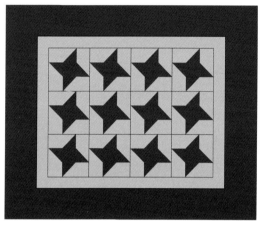

Straight borders

These are the most popular of borders as they are the easiest to make. Using un-patterned fabric gives a clean border to your design and neatly frames it.

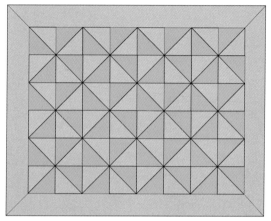

Mitred borders

Again, using an un-patterned fabric, this can give a neat and clean border to your design. However, with cutting the corners at a 45-degree angle, these mitred borders provide a more professional finish to your work.

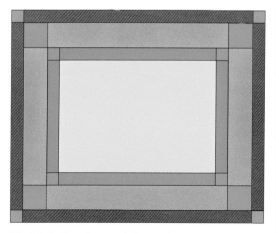

Multiple borders with setting squares

You don't need to stop at one border, adding two or more together in different colours and widths with contrasting setting squares is best used on larger projects, like quilts or throws.

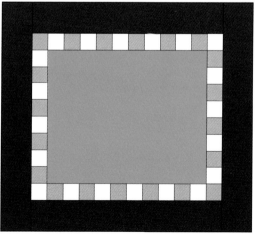

Pieced inner border with straight outer border

Straight borders mixed with a pieced patchwork border gives more interest to your work, with one border framing another.

Make straight borders

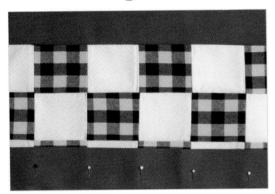

01 Cut and pin the edges

Cut two strips of fabric of the required width plus ½in (1.2cm) seam allowance and of equal length to the side of the quilt you are matching it to. Mark with a pin, the centre of the strips and the edge of your quilt, match these with fabric right sides together and continue to pin the rest of the edge then sew using a ¼in (6mm) seam allowance. Press the seams to the border strip.

02 Add the end strips

Measure the width of the top and bottom edges of your quilt incorporating the borders, cut two more strips to this length and the same width as your first strips. Mark the centres of the strip and quilt edge, and follow as in Step 1.

03 Now move on to the next stage

Your quilt is now complete and ready to be used in the next stage of your project.

Join strips to make a border

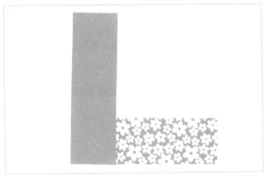

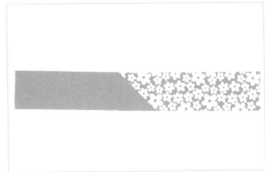

01 Pin the strips together

Position two fabric strips, right sides together at right angles to each other. Overlap the ends by at least ¼in (6mm). Draw your diagonal line, pin the two strips together and sew along this line.

02 Trim and sew the edges

Trim off the excess material at the ¼in (6mm) seam line and trim at the strip edges if necessary. Press your seam to one side.

Making a straight border with setting squares

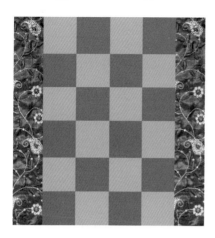

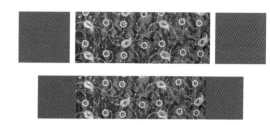

02 Measure and cut the ends

Measure and cut two strips of fabric for the next two sides of your patchwork, only measure for the actual patchwork piece and not include the borders you have just worked, including your ½in (1.2cm) seam allowance.

01 Attach the edges

Measure and cut two strips of fabric for two sides of your patchwork (incorporating your ½in (1.2cm) seam allowance) — see Step 1 of 'Making straight borders'. Pin these strips to either side of your patchwork and sew. Press seams of your patchwork towards the border strip.

03 Cut the squares

Now, cut four setting squares, the width should match the width of your border strips. Then with right sides together, pin and sew a square to either end of your border strips. Press your seams to the longer border strip.

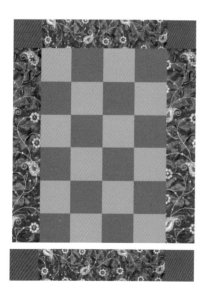

04 Pin and sew the ends

Place your border strips, with right sides together, along the bottom and top edges of your work, taking care to match up your seams in the corners, pin and sew. Press your seams towards the border.

05 Move onto the next stage

Your top part of your quilt cover is now complete. All that is left to do is attach it to the back and finish off.

Making a mitred border

01 Measure and cut

Square up your quilt edge, by trimming any uneven pieces. Decide how wide you want your border to be, then add this measurement twice to the width of your quilt plus seam allowance of ½in (1.2cm) twice for each side. Cut 4 border strips of this width and length.

02 Pin and mark the seam allowance

Position a pin in both the centre of the border strip and the edge of the quilted piece. With right sides together, match these two pins and continue to pin your border strip to your quilt. Mark your seam allowance at either end of your quilt at ¼in (6mm) — this denotes your start and finish points for your sewing line.

03 Sew the border strip

Sew your border strips to your quilt, ensuring you leave a ¼in (6mm) seam allowance at either side of the quilt edge — do not stitch into adjacent strips. Press all seams towards the border strips.

04 Pin and press

With your quilt face-up, fold under your border strips at 45-degree angles (use your quilter's ruler if it helps). Once correct, pin in place and press these folds, remove your pins, turn over your quilt and re-pin on the wrong side.

05 Hand sew and trim

If it helps, tack your border in place, then hand sew the fold together, starting at the quilt corner and working your way outwards. Trim off your seam allowance and press your seams open. Repeat this method for all your remaining corners.

Multiple mitred borders

Join strips of fabric together

If you wish to make a multiple mitred border, join strips of fabric together in one piece before attaching to your quilt — it is not necessary for these strips to be of the same width, but ensure you make them wide enough to allow for this extra wide border. Following steps 4-5, attach to your quilt — ensure you match your mitred border seams as you go, then press your seams open.

Curves

Even though working with straight edges offers lots of variety, there's even more you can do when you add curves to your patchwork

While they might look daunting to sew, don't be put off using curves. Adding them to your patchwork will open up many new options for patterns, and they aren't as difficult as you might think. One of the most important things when sewing curves is to carefully prepare every stage, from template making and cutting to pinning. This will make things easier when it comes to finally sewing them all together. You may find that you prefer hand stitching when it comes to working with curves, but machine stitching works just as well.

Sewing curved seams by hand

01 Mark the seamlines

Begin by marking the seamlines and registration marks on the wrong side of every piece. It is especially important to mark the centre point. If this is not marked on the pattern you are following, find it by folding each piece in half and fingerpressing the piece along the centre seamline. Use this crease as the centre mark.

02 Pin the pieces

Line the pieces up by placing the smaller, convex piece on the large concave one with the right sides facing each other. Make sure the edges and the centre creases of both pieces align. Pin together, starting with the aligned centre mark and then the end points of the marked seamline. Pin along the seamline regularly. Eliminate creases in the fabric as you go.

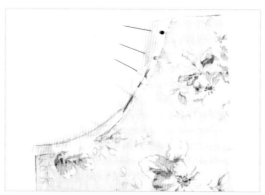

03 Sew together

Remove the pin at one end and take the needle through the marks left by the pin. Secure the thread using a double back-stitched loop in the seamline. Sew along the seamline taking several short running stitches, then pull the needle through. Repeat along the length of the seam, removing pins as you work. If you want to secure the seam further, make a small back stitch each time you bring the needle through. Do not sew into the seam allowance.

04 Press

Before you finish sewing, check to make sure your stitching is on the lines on both sides and stops at the matching point at the ends. If it is, secure with a back-stitched loop. Do not trim the seam allowance. Press the seam towards the convex piece, and it should lie flat.

Sewing curved seams by machine

01 Mark seamlines and centre mark

If you are making your own templates, make sure you mark the centre line on each. Cut out your fabric allowing for a ¼in (6mm) seam allowance. Centre your templates on the wrong side of your fabric and draw around them to mark the seamlines. Also mark on the fabric where the centre point is.

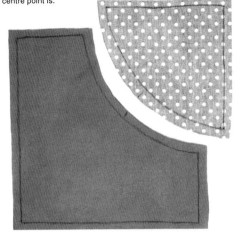

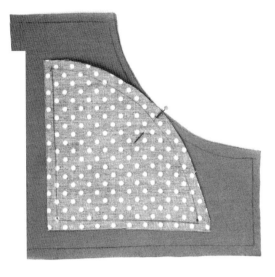

02 Pin together

Pin your pieces together starting at the centre mark. Pin at each end, then along the seamline.

Reducing bulk

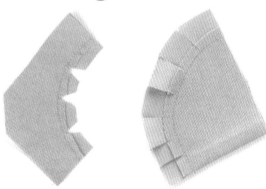

01 Reduce bulk on the inner curve

If your patchwork isn't lying flat, you may need to reduce the seam bulk. Layer the seam by cutting along one side of the seam allowance, aiming to reduce it to one-third of its original width. Add V-shaped notches at regular intervals to remove bulk.

03 Sew

Stitch along the seamline, removing the pins as you go. Be careful not to stretch or pull either piece of fabric while you're working. Press when you are done.

02 Reduce bulk on the outer curve

Layer the seam and clip through the seam allowances to reduce bulk.

Fans

01 Make two sets of templates

When cutting out your templates, make two sets: one for the cutting lines and one with the seam allowances trimmed off the curved edges for the stitching line.

02 Cut your pieces

To make a six-blade fan, cut three blades from Fabrics A and B. Cut a corner piece from Fabric C and a background piece from Fabric D.

05 Join small corner piece

Line up the centre marks of the bottom edge of the fan and the small corner piece, and pin together on the centre mark. Pin the edges and at regular intervals along the curve. Sew together using one of the methods on the previous page. Press towards the fan.

03 Join the fan blades

Join the six fan blade pieces taking a ¼in (6mm) seam allowance, making sure all the smaller ends are at the same edge. Alternate the fabrics to form the pattern. Press the blades in one direction.

04 Mark seam allowance

On the fan you just created, mark a ¼in (6mm) seam allowance on the top and bottom edges. Also mark a ¼in (6mm) seam allowance on the small corner piece.

06 Join the background piece

Mark a ¼in (6mm) seam allowance and the centre mark on the background piece. Pin the background piece to the top edge of the fan piece as before. Sew as before. Press towards the background piece. Voila! You made a patchwork fan.

Drunkard's Path

01 Two templates

When cutting out your templates, make two sets: one for the cutting lines and one with the seam allowances trimmed off the curved edges for the stitching line. Place the registration marks precisely on both sets.

02 Trace outlines

Precisely trace the outlines of your larger templates on to the wrong side of your chosen fabric and transfer the registration marks.

03 Cut out shapes

If you are using a rotary cutter, use the smallest blade you have available for precision. Make sure to cut around the curve and not into it.

 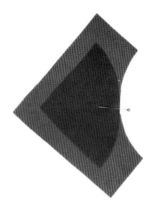 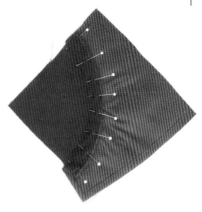

04 Trace seam allowances

Place your second set of templates (the ones with the seam allowances removed) on to the fabric and trace around them to mark the seamlines. Make sure you make your marks on the wrong side of the fabric.

05 Place together

Take one of each size piece and then place together with the right sides facing. Make sure that the convex piece is on top of the concave one. Now pin the centre marks together.

06 Pin along seamline

Place pins at both seamline edges, then at regular intervals along the seamline. Manipulate the fabric as you go in order to get rid of lumps and bumps.

08 Press

Carefully press your finished squares. You shouldn't find that you need to trim the curves.

07 Stitch together

Stitch along the seamlines, either by hand or machine, removing the pins as you go. It may save time if you pin all 16 pieces you need first, then you can concentrate on sewing them in one go.

TOP TIP
If your curved blocks aren't quite square, simply trim all four sides by the same amount to keep your pattern central.

09 Make pattern

Sew your finished squares into four rows of four to make the Drunkard's Path pattern. Press the seams on opposite directions on alternate rows.

10 Join

Sew together the four rows, matching the seams carefully. Now press.

English paper piecing

Have fun with mosaic patterns using this technique

This is a traditional way of making a quilt of mosaic shapes. The fabric pieces — which can be any shape with at least two bias edges — are tacked to pre-cut templates. This technique is usually carried out by hand, and the backing papers can be cut from virtually any heavy paper. People often use freezer paper, as it can be ironed on quickly and is easy to remove.

"People often use freezer paper, as it can be ironed on quickly and is easy to remove"

Basic paper-piecing technique

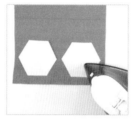

01 Draw around template
Make a template, unless you are using pre-cut shapes. Draw around it multiple times and then cut out using paper scissors.

02 Attach template
Pin a paper shape or iron a freezer paper shape to the wrong side of the fabric, leaving enough space for seam allowances.

03 Cut out
Cut out each shape (including the seam allowance) from the fabric using either fabric scissors or a rotary cutter. Take care to keep at least one side of the shape along the straight grain of the fabric.

04 Fold over
Fold the seam allowance over the wrong side of the paper shape, folding each corner neatly, and tack along the edges to hold the fabric in place.

05 Stitch together
To stitch units together, place two shapes with the right sides together. Continue by making a back-stitched loop and oversewing to the corner as close to the fold as possible. Be careful not to sew through the backing papers.

06 Go back
Oversew along the same edge to the opposite corner, taking small stitches and only stitching through fabric. When you reach the opposite corner, back stitch for ¼in (6mm).

07 Repeat until finished
Continuing adding shapes until the final shape is completed. If you need to reuse the papers, you can remove them once all the shapes adjoining a particular piece have been added by clipping the tacking stitches and gently pulling the paper out.

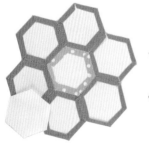
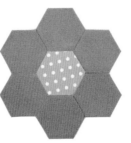

Setting in hexagons

01 Add a third
Set a third hexagon by oversewing one side of the seam, starting at the centre point.

02 Fold if needed
Align the second sides to join them at their outer points by folding back the pieces as necessary. Continue stitching to hold in place.

Neat folds

01 Crisp press
Make a neat fold at the sharp points when tacking diamonds and triangles by sewing in the middle of one side. When you reach the point, finger press the extended seam allowance.

02 Keep stitching
Fold over the allowance from the next side, and then take the stitch through the fold and continue, but do not trim off the fabric extensions.

Neat joins

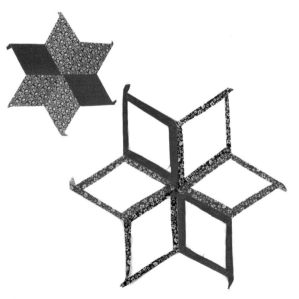

01 To the side
To make a neat join while sewing pieces together, fold the extension to the side so you don't stitch through them. The unstitched extensions will form a spiral around their meeting point in the centre.

Strip piecing

Use cut strips for interesting patterns

S trip piecing is the method of attaching long strips of material together by either joining or piecing, then cutting them using a rotary cutter into blocks and re-joining in a pattern. Log cabin projects (see page 82) can be made using this method in addition to seminole patchwork (see page 90). Rail Fence block work is a flexible quilt block method that can be used to create multiple designs both traditional and modern depending on your choice of fabric. Strip piecing is an easy way of adding fun to your quilt.

Cut and join

01 Attach the strips

Using different and complementing fabrics, cut three strips of the same width. Select strips 1 and 2 and with right sides together, sew along the length using a ¼in (6mm) seam allowance. When joining your third strip, change the direction of sewing, this will prevent any puckering or bowing. Press your seams away from the centre strip.

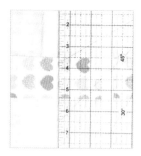

02 Cut squares

Measure the width of your pieced strip and use this measurement to cut squares this size across your pieced strip using your quilter's ruler and rotary cutter.

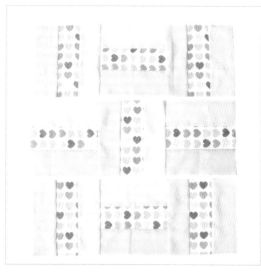

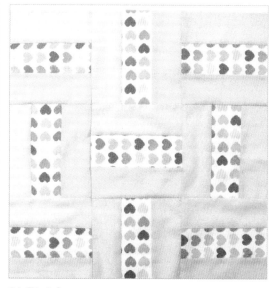

03 Build the pattern

Lay out your pieced squares to form three rows in the pattern shown. Select one row and with right sides together and using a ¼in (6mm) seam allowance, sew the three squares together. Repeat for all three rows. Press your seams to one side, alternate the direction for each row.

04 Finish up

Match your pieced units right sides together, ensuring your seams match up and pin to hold in place. Sew, leaving a ¼in (6mm) seam allowance. Press seams open.

String piecing

If you prefer a more relaxed effect, try this out

String piecing involves piecing together uneven straight strips of fabric into a block. These string-pieced blocks can be made in any size and used with other units to form a larger piece of work. Using fabric with contrasting colours and patterns will give the best results. Use seam allowances of ¼in (6mm) and if using a paper foundation block, as in method 2, increase your stitch length to 1.5in — this will make it easier to remove the paper block when complete. A muslin foundation will remain in place.

Method 1

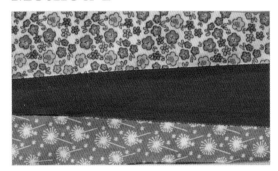

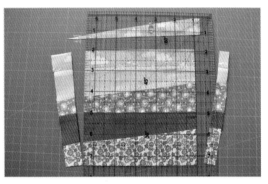

01 Attach two strings

With your strings of fabric selected, take two and pin with right sides together, sew allowing for your seam allowance. To prevent any bowing, turn your work each time you sew on a new string.

02 Press to finish

Before trimming to size using your rotary cutter and quilter's ruler, press all seams in one direction.

Method 2

01 Foundation block

Cut a paper or muslin foundation block to size, allowing for the seam. With right side up, place the first string in the middle of the block, take the second string, align and pin on top of the first, right side down. It's important the strings are longer than the block itself. Sew through all layers along your seam allowance line. Turn and press the seams outwards.

02 New seam

Add a new string to the opposite edge of the first string, then sew as in Step 1. Turn and press the seams outwards.

03 Repeat and press

Continue in this way until your foundation block is completely covered, ensuring you press the seams as you go. Cut off the excess material surrounding the foundation. If using a paper foundation, allow for your seam allowance before trimming.

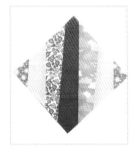

04 Final press

If using a paper foundation, carefully tear it away from the fabric. If using a muslin foundation, it will not be removed from the final piece. Press all seams.

Log cabin

Have a go at this ancient and traditional quilt design

og cabin is a visually attractive block design and has been used in quilts for hundreds of years. It is most commonly made using fabric strips that are built around a central square unit, you can, however, start with other central shapes. The blocks can be chain pieced or made individually. Always use a ¼in (6mm) seam allowance unless stated otherwise.

Method 1: Individual blocks

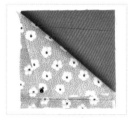

01 Square block

Starting with a central square block, cut another in Fabric A of the same size. Place right sides together and sew using a ¼in (6mm) seam allowance down one edge. Press seams open.

02 Another square

Cut a second strip of Fabric A that is the same width as the central square, but the length of your pieced unit. With right sides together, sew this strip to your pieced unit on the long side.

03 Keep working

Cut two strips from Fabric B, following the method in Step 2 and sew to your unit. Work clockwise around your central square. For guidance, follow the 1-13 step guide on page 160.

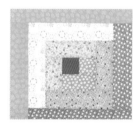

04 Build it up

Follow in this manner, adding two strips from either the same two fabric colours or differing ones. Continue working clockwise until you have reached the required size block.

Method 2: Courthouse Steps variation

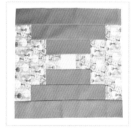

01 Pieced unit

Cut a central square of fabric and two more of the same size in Fabric A. Sew these two pieces to opposite sides of your central square, with right sides together and using a ¼in (6mm) seam allowance, creating a pieced unit. Press your seams away from the central square.

02 Surround strips

Using the same width as your original square, cut two more strips from Fabric B the same length as the long side of the pieced unit. Sew these two strips to the long sides of your original unit, on opposite sides. Press your seams away from the centre unit.

03 Keep going

Continue as in Step 2, adding two strips of Fabric A to the top, then Fabric B to the sides until you reach the required block size. Press all seams away from the centre as you sew on each strip.

Method 3: Chain piecing

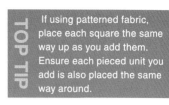
Chain piecing is the method of sewing pieces together against one longer piece without stopping or cutting as you go. You can sew any number together, which will save time and thread as well as avoiding any bunched or puckered seams. It is a very useful technique if you need to make many pieces exactly the same, especially in block piecing.

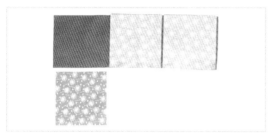

01 Centre squares

Taking Fabric A, cut as many centre squares as needed including your seam allowance in the measurement. With Fabric B, cut strips the same width as the Fabric A squares. With right sides together, place your first centre square at the end of your strip and sew, leaving a ¼in (6mm) seam allowance.

02 Create the chain

As you reach the end of sewing your first centre square to your strip, add your second square, leaving a small space between this and your first, and carry on sewing. Continue in this way until all squares have been sewn to your strip. This creates a chain of units.

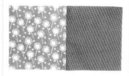

03 Now cut

Cut the units apart; trim away any excess material to ensure all squares are the same size. Press the seams open.

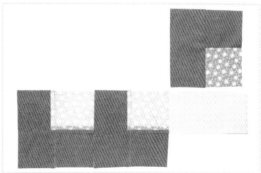

04 Work in threes

With a second Fabric B strip, attach your opened pieced units right sides together along the strip. Ensure that you keep your units the same way round, ie, keep Fabric A squares below Fabric B squares. As before, sew your first pieced unit on this strip, then add your second pieced unit and continue until you have made several three-part units. Press seams.

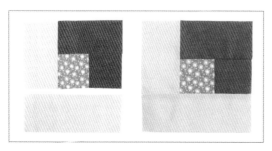

05 Introduce Fabric C

Cut a strip of Fabric C using the width of original Fabric A squares. With right sides together, place the first of your three-part units on Fabric C, ensuring you keep the Fabric A square at the bottom. Sew your first unit, then add your second without lifting your needle from the fabric. Continue until all units are sewn, cut, trim excess and press seams.

06 Keep clockwise

Repeat this process to add your fourth strip of Fabric C, attaching it to the last unstitched side of the Fabric A square. Repeat this process adding two strips of alternating B, C and A fabrics until your block is complete. Always work clockwise as you attach each strip.

Foundation paper piecing

Achieve sharp points and precise piecing with this technique

When the pieces in a quilt block are too complicated to cut through traditional rotary cutting methods, foundation paper piecing helps you achieve perfect results every time. All you need to do is sew along pre-printed lines! Aligning your fabrics is the hardest part of this method, so make sure to cut pieces that are plenty large until you get the hang of it.

Simple continuous sashing

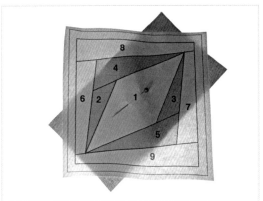

01 Prepare your templates

Print or copy the paper templates, ensuring that the size has not been distorted during printing. Double-check this by measuring the template itself (it should measure the same as the unfinished block), or using the sizing test box that many patterns provide. Print the templates on lightweight copy paper or on paper designed especially for paper piecing, which is typically similar to newsprint.

02 Place the first piece of fabric

Cut a piece of fabric that generously covers the area marked 1 on the template. There should be at least 3/8in-½in (1-1.2cm) excess fabric on all sides. Using a pin or a small dab of water-soluble glue, secure the fabric to the paper template, ensuring that the wrong side of the fabric is facing the blank, unprinted side of the paper template (ie not covering up the visible lines).

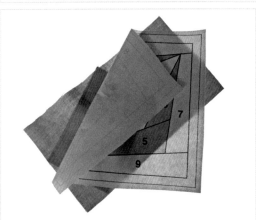

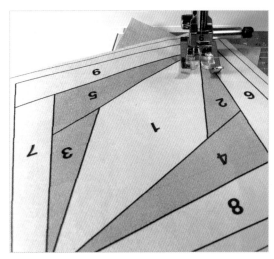

03 Align the second piece of fabric

Fold back the paper along the line between areas 1 and 2. It may help to place an index card along the line and then fold the paper back along the edge. With the paper folded back along the line between areas 1 and 2, align your next piece of fabric. Place fabric 2 right sides together with fabric 1, and hold the paper up to the light to ensure that it generously covers area 2 on the paper template (there should be about ⅜in-½in (1-1.2cm) excess on all sides). Place a pin to hold fabric 2 in place.

04 Sew along the marked line

Unfold and flatten out the paper template, leaving the fabrics as they are. Reduce the stitch length to about 1.5mm, and sew along the marked line between areas 1 and 2. Begin and end stitching about ¼in before and after the lines.

05 Trim the seam

Gently fold fabric 2 back with your fingers and double-check that it now covers area 2 on the unfolded paper template with at least ¼in (6mm) excess on all unsewn sides. If so, fold the paper template back again along your newly sewn seam and trim the seam allowance of fabric 2 to ¼in (6mm) using an Add-A-Quarter ruler or the 1/4in (6mm) line on your standard rotary cutting ruler. (If not, remove the seam, realign the fabric, and sew again).

06 Press the seam

Open up the paper template and press fabric 2 back along the visible stitched line.

TOP TIP

When replacing your normal rotary blade, switch it to a cutter kept just for paper piecing, since trimming through paper will dull your new blade more quickly.

07 Continue adding fabrics

Repeat Steps 3-6, adding fabrics in numerical order. When folding back the foundation paper, you may have to gently pull the paper away from any stitching in the seam allowance. It should come away easily thanks to the shortened stitch length, but it is still a good idea to hold the thread ends of your seam when pulling away.

08 Trim the block to size

When you have completed the block by adding all fabrics, trim the block along the outside lines using a ruler.

09 Remove the foundation papers

Remove the foundation papers by gently pulling them away from the seam, starting with the outside edges. If any small pieces prove difficult to remove, use tweezers to help you grip them.

Folded patchwork

Create stunning patchwork blocks by folding your fabric in these different ways

Some of the most interesting patchwork patterns can be achieved by folding fabric — either one layer or several different types — in different ways before piecing the blocks together. And because these pieces are for more than one layer, they are especially good in quilts as they can add definition, texture and warmth to your creation. Your fingerpress and your iron will be some of your most important tools for this technique, as pressing is crucial to achieve the clean lines you'll need for your patchwork blocks. You'll need at least two fabrics for each design. Follow these steps to create beautifully folded patchwork creations!

Cathedral window

01 Measure and cut

Choose the size that you want your finished patchwork square to be and then double it. Add a ½in (1.2cm) seam allowance, then cut 4 squares of the same size out of your background fabric.

02 Find the centre

Fold in the seam allowance and press to make clean-cut edges. Fold the square in half diagonally one way and press to make a crease. Unfold and then fold in half diagonally the other way. Press to make a crease. Unfold. The centre of the square will be where the two creases meet.

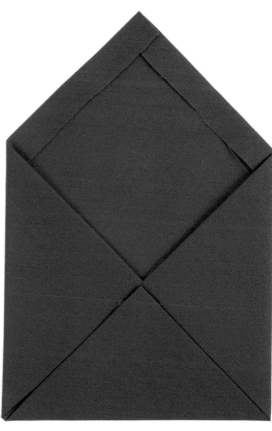

03 Fold corners in

Fold each corner of the square in to the centre, lining it up with the creases you just made. Press to make sure the new corners of the square are sharply defined.

04 Secure

To secure the points in place, take a cross stitch through each point, making sure to go through all the layers.

05 Fold corners in again

Bring each corner in to the centre as before and press firmly. Make a cross stitch through all the points to hold in place. Make sure to go through all the layers. Your square will now be your original intended size. Make 3 more squares in the same way.

06 Join four squares together

With the folded edges facing each other, sew together 2 squares along one edge with tiny stitches. Sew together the other 2 in the same way. Join the 2 pairs to make a square.

07 Cut contrast windows

Out of your contrasting fabric, cut four windows, each of which should just fit inside a quarter segment of the background square. To work out the size, measure from the centre of one of the folded squares to the outside corner.

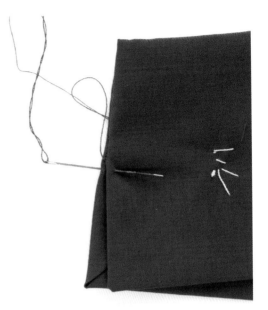

08 Place windows

Your windows will go over a seam on the diagonal. Place the first and secure with pins. Trim any excess at this time if they are not quite the right size.

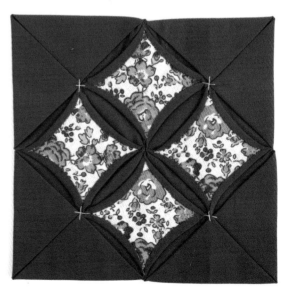

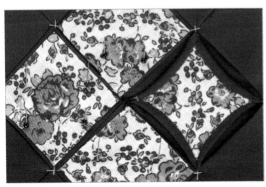

09 Roll the edges

Roll the folded edges of one of your background squares over the raw edges of its window.

10 Stitch together

Using thread to match your background fabric, sew the roll to the window with tiny stitches. Make sure not to stitch through the background fabric. Repeat on the other three edges of the window.

Secret garden

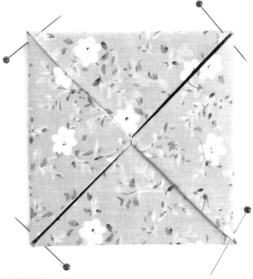

01 Make a folded square

Follow Steps 1-3 of the cathedral window tutorial to make a folded square out of your background fabric. Fold and press as in Step 4, but do not stitch in place. Cut a window square in your contrasting fabric that is the same size as your folded square.

02 Place window

Open out the unstitched corners of your background square and place the window square on point within the lines. Trim the square if there's any overhang. Anchor with small tacking stitches.

03 Fold in the corners

Covering the contrast window, fold in the 4 corners of your background square to meet at the centre. Secure the points by stitching a small cross in the centre, going through all points and all layers.

04 Pin

Place pins in each corner of the square, ¼in (6mm) in from the corner edge. This will stabilise all the layers of the square.

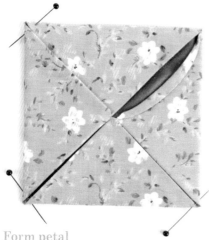

05 Form petal

Fold over one diagonal edge of the background square to form a curving petal shape that allows the contrast window to show through. Starting at the centre, sew in place using thread to match the background fabric.

06 Repeat and finish

Repeat step 5 on the further seven diagonal edges of the square to form the petal shapes. Remove the pins and secure each corner with a double tacking stitch. Press to finish.

Folded star

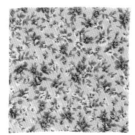
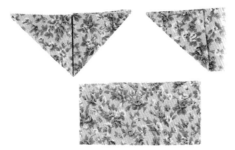

01 Calico base

This fun quilted star is made using a calico foundation square with 4 other layers, or rounds of triangles on top. Cut the calico to your finished size, plus 2in (5cm) and then 12 4in (10cm) squares from fabric A for rounds 1 and 3, and 16 4in (10cm)§ squares from fabric B for rounds 2 and 4.

02 Press in half

To make the triangles, press each square in half with the wrong sides together. Fold one top corner of the rectangle you have just made to the centre of the raw edges and press. Repeat with the opposite top corner to make two right-angle triangles back to back.

03 Fold and press

Fold the foundation square in half horizontally and vertically and then press to make the guidelines. Fold along the diagonals and press again. Open it up.

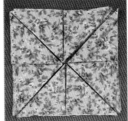

04 Tack and attach

To complete round 1, place the 4 fabric A triangles along the guidelines you created so their points meet at the centre. Tack them into place and secure each point with a small hidden stitch.

05 Place triangles

For round 2, place 4 fabric B triangles on the piece with their points ⅜ in (1cm) from the centre and with their edges in line with the sides of the calico foundation square. Tack and sew to secure as before and add 4 more triangles with their flat edges aligning with the diagonal pressed guides you made in Step 2.

06 Layer it up

Layer 8 fabric A triangles for round 2 and 8 fabric B triangles for round 4. Tack and attach them as required.

Seminole

Learn the patchwork style used by the Native American Seminole tribe

Seminole patchwork originated from the Seminole tribe of Native Americans back in the late 1800s. Originally the women used fabric from the end of bolts to create what was known as "strip clothing". These can be used for borders or block-work and are created by cutting pieced strips at an angle and then re-joining them to create simple or elaborate patterns. Seminole patchwork was used for traditional dress: long skirts for women and patchwork shirts for men. You will still see people wear these today on special occasions.

Method 1: Straight band

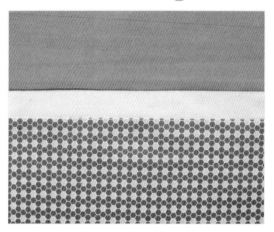

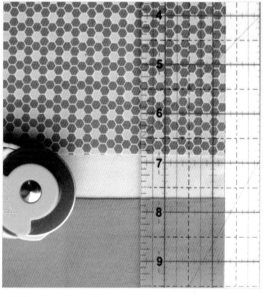

01 Cut your fabric

Cut strips from 3 contrasting fabrics with differing widths, allowing for a ¼in (6mm) seam allowances on each piece. The picture is using the ratio of 2:1:3, this is to allow the centre line to be evenly offset in the finished work. With right sides together, join the 3 strips. Press the seams away from the lighter strip.

02 Use your quilters ruler

Cut across the joined piece to give yourself different widths, using a quilters ruler and rotary cutter. Don't forget to include your ¼in (6mm) seam allowance.

03 Organise your cuts

Once cut, alternate each cut piece top-to-bottom and arrange your pieces in your desired pattern. Then with right sides together, sew the strips together leaving ¼in (6mm) seam allowance. Once finished, press all seams in the same direction.

TOP TIP Pressing the seams away from the lighter colour means the darker colours won't show through on the finished item.

Method 2: Angled band

01 Cut your fabric

Cut three strips of varying widths from contrasting fabric.

02 Sew the cuts together

Sew together, placing the narrow strip in the middle of the two wider bands. Press the seams in one direction.

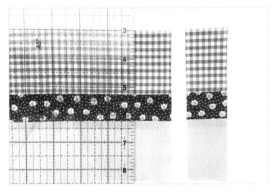

03 Use your quilters ruler

Cut across the joined strip using your quilters ruler and rotary cutter, making pieced strips of your required width.

04 Use your seam allowance

Sew together using a ¼in (6mm) seam allowance; offset your centre square as you join each strip together. Press your seams in one direction.

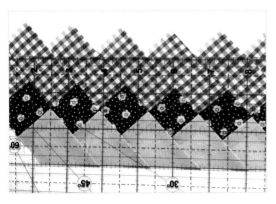

05 Trim the edges

Use a rotary cutter and quilters ruler to trim off the points on both sides of the strip.

06 Tidy and finish

Trim off at both ends of this pieced strip to square up and create a neat pieced strip.

Method 3: Chevron band

Chevron quilting creates fun zig-zag designs that look complicated, but are very straightforward to make.

You can make large or small chevrons, using just two different fabrics or use up scraps to make a fun patchwork.

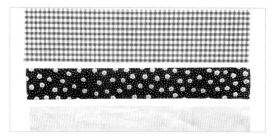

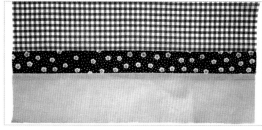

01 Cut your fabric

From contrasting fabrics, cut three strips of the same width, with right sides together, sew the first two strips together; turn your work to sew in the opposite direction to attach your second strip. Press seams in one direction. Repeat to make a second matching strip.

02 Cut into strips

Using the 45 degree angle on your quilters ruler make your first cut across one of the pieced strips using a rotary cutter. Cut several strips to your required width, including the provision of your seam allowance of ½in (1.2cm).

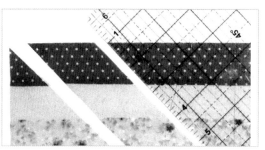

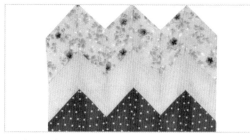

04 Sew the strips together

Take one cut piece from each pieced strip and match up seams, pin and sew together using a ¼in (6mm) seam allowance. Repeat process to join strips into pairs.

03 And now the other way

Repeat as in Step 2 for the second pieced strip. However, cut your 45-degree angle in the opposite direction.

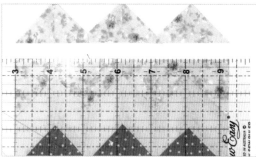

05 Trim and tidy

Continue to sew together the paired pieces to create a chevron band. Press seams in one direction. Using a quilters ruler and rotary cutter, trim the points off from either end.

06 End result

Your finished piece creates a chevron band across your pieced strip, ready to add to a larger piece or use on its own.

Quilting

Add to your know-how and start adding to your items

"Straight, even stitches are worked, ideally with the needle at an angle of 90 degrees"

Transfer designs

Clever methods for copying your quilting designs

T ransferring a quilting pattern to a quilt can be a little tricky, but there are several methods you can try to speed up the process. Mark the fabric with something that can easily be removed, like water or air-soluble pens or tailor's chalk, you can easily draw on your designs, or copy something else. Here we take you through a couple of different examples.

Masking tape

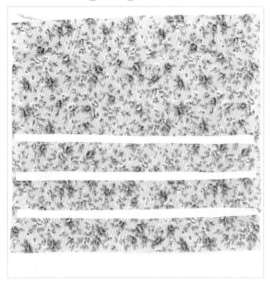

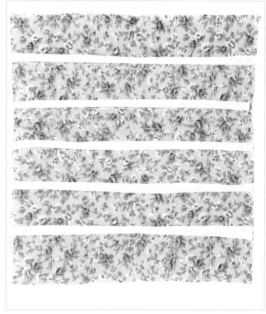

01 Mark out the lines

With your quilt laid out on a flat surface, lay out your masking tape strips parallel to the edges of your fabric at equal distances.

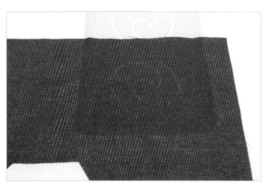

02 Stitch and rip

Using your tape as a guide, sew along the lines using your preferred method of stitching — by hand or using your machine. Remove the tape when you're done and place stripes at a 90-degree angle ready to do the same again, but the other way.

Tracing

01 Make use of light

If the fabric you are using is light enough, you could place it over a lightbox with the pattern you wish to trace beneath it and draw over the pattern with a fabric pencil. Alternatively, you can place a bulb beneath a glass table-top and create your own lightbox. Or lie a sheet of Perspex across a level raised surface with a bulb beneath.

Templates or stencils

01 Tape the design

Make your quilt sandwich with your material and your wadding. Tape your templated pattern to the top of the material with masking tape, ready to draw. Keeping to the template as closely as possible, draw around it with a very sharp pencil.

02 Move along

Repeat the pattern as desired by moving the template and re-fixing it to the fabric and draw around it again. Do so as much as you like.

Trace and track

01 Sew it on

If your material is particularly difficult to mark, or pencil lines simply won't show up, draw your design onto tissue paper and pin it into place. Sew along the drawn line as required.

02 Carefully remove

Once you're happy with the stitching, carefully peel away the tissue paper, making sure not to snag the stitches you have made. Ripping the paper more is better than pulling too hard on the stitches.

Hand quilting basics

Learn the fundamentals of hand quilting and take your work anywhere!

To give your quilt a softer look, have a go at quilting by hand. Straight, even stitches are worked, ideally with the needle at an angle of 90 degrees. The aim is to have the same stitch length on the front and back. To get around the thickness of the quilt layers, we stitch using a technique known as 'rocking' the needle, which requires the use of both hands.

While quilting by hand, use quilting threads and needles, and wear a thimble on your middle finger and a protective guard underneath.

Knotting to begin

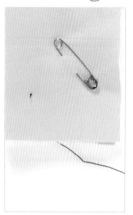

01 First stitch

Tie a knot at the end of a 20in (50cm) length of quilting thread. Pull the needle down through the top layer of fabric, about 1in (2.5cm) away from where you wish to start stitching. Bring it out where you intend to begin.

02 Pull until it pops

Gently pull the thread until the knot pops through the top layer of the fabric but not hard enough to bring it out again. The knot should end up burying itself in the wadding, becoming virtually undetectable.

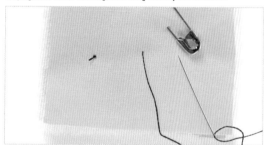

Finishing off

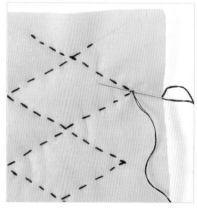

01 Back on yourself

To secure the thread at the end, do a small backstitch through the top layer and pull the thread through. Make a French knot close to the end of the stitching, secure it with your finger, and pull the knot tight.

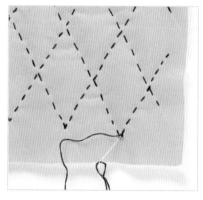

02 French knot

Push the needle point through only the top layer next to where the thread emerges and in the opposite direction to the rest of the stitching. Slide the needle into the wadding and pull it out about ¾in (2cm) from the end of the stitching. Pull the French knot through into the wadding.

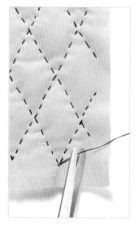

03 Tail sink

Cut off the thread close to the surface of the quilt and let the tail sink into the wadding.

Quilting or rocking stitch

01 Hand position

Working inside a large embroidery hoop, bury a knot into a quilt sandwich. Place one hand under the quilt where the needle should emerge.

02 Feel the point

With the needle between your thumb and forefinger, push the needle with your thimbled finger straight down until you feel the point with your underneath hand.

03 Match lengths

With your underneath finger, start to push up gently against the side of the needle and the quilt. At the same time, push down with your thumb and make a lump in the layers while you push the needle sideways back through to the top. Stop pushing when the length of the needle protruding on the top is the same length of the next stitch.

> **TOP TIP**
> Use cotton threads when stitching older fabrics as synthetic threads may cut or damage the fabric.

04 Break through

Bring the eye of the needle upright again using the thimbled finger, while at the same time pushing in front of it with your thumb. Then push down as in Step 1 when the needle is upright and the point breaks through the fabric.

05 Repeat to finish

Continue the motion until the needle has as many stitches as it will hold, and then pull the needle and thread all the way through.

Stab stitch

01 Bury the knot

Stab stitch is an alternative way of working on thick quilts. Working inside a large hoop as above and using a thimble on each middle finder, bury the knot as in 'Knotting to begin'. Push the upright needle straight down through all the layers, and pull the needle and thread through to the back.

02 Keep going

Push the upright needle back up through all the layers within the embroidery hoop, working a stitch length away from the previous stitch. Pull the needle and thread through the top. Repeat as needed.

Machine quilting basics

Utilise your machine to make beautifully quilted blankets

W hile hand-quilting your project can be good fun, you can also use your machine to add the quilting details. Some people believe machine quilting to be second best to hand quilting, but this is simply untrue. Both have their positives, and quilting using your machine will offer an even finish, and machine-quilted blankets are often flatter as well.

Prepare your quilt

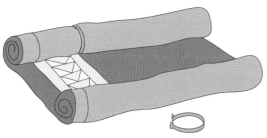
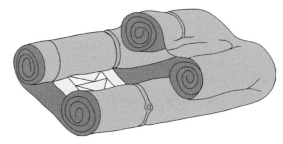

01 Grip the edges

Working small areas at a time, roll up both sides of your quilt towards the centre. Leave 12in (30cm) in the middle, and grip the edges with clips.

02 Secure it all

Secure the other ends of the quilt and work your way around until it is all secured.

Grid patterns

The most traditional way you can detail your quilt is using grid patterns, in either square or diamond shapes. Mark your grid lines with your fabric pen or pencil, and follow them as you go.

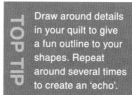

TOP TIP
Draw around details in your quilt to give a fun outline to your shapes. Repeat around several times to create an 'echo'.

01 Watch the angle

Line up your guides and stitch your first marked row. Using this, now measure out your following rows. To create diamonds, make sure you angle your work so the edge is at 45 degrees to the machine.

02 Be square

Turn your quilt by 90 degrees and repeat the process the other way to achieve squares or rectangles.

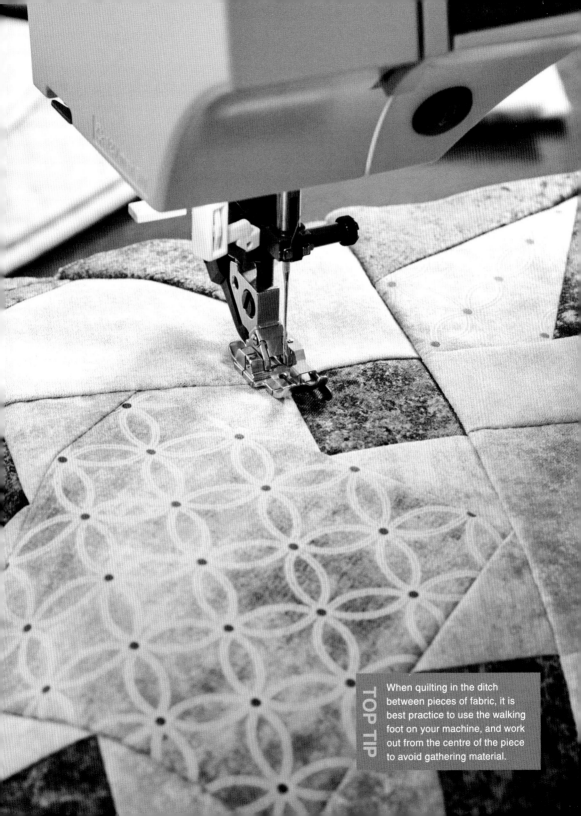

Corded quilting and trapunto

Sprinkle some dimensional magic on your quilts

Corded quilting (Italian quilting) and trapunto (or stuffed quilting) are decorative techniques where the outline is usually worked by hand sewing. These methods can be used together or separately, but used together they give a beautiful 3D finish to your quilting project. Both methods require you to have a top fabric layer and thinner backing layer (which is generally butter muslin). The motif is then filled from the back using either cord, stuffing material or knitting wool.

Create another dimension

01 Trace the design

Cut your main fabric and trace your design to the right side. Use a water-soluble pen or pencil mark that will come out with washing. Cut a piece of muslin to the same size as your main fabric, then tack these together around your design.

02 Sew the design

Hand sew the outline of your motif with a running stitch. Where any lines meet, make sure to keep your stitches separate so they do not cross over. When you've finished, remove the outline markings.

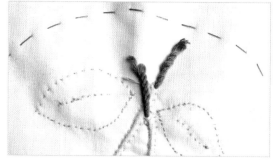

03 Insert cord or wool

Select your soft cord or knitting wool and thread onto a tapestry needle. On the reverse side of your work, push your needle through the first layer of muslin and along the stem line of your work. Leave a short tail at either end.

04 Stuff it

Still on the reverse side, cut a small slit in the middle of the backing layer of each section to be filled. Gently work small pieces of stuffing into the hole, but don't overfill. Repeat for each section to be filled.

05 Close when finished

To close each of these slits, use a crossed stitch, such as herringbone. Also cross stitch over the ends of the cord lengths to secure these in place, and then trim off the excess.

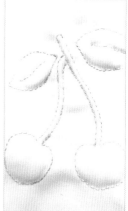

06 Finish up

Remove the tacking stitch surrounding your work. Cording and trapunto gives a 3D effect to your finished piece.

Tying

Tying is a method used in quilting to hold the layers of the quilt together without using long runs of cotton across the fabric. You can use whatever you like to achieve this effect, be it cotton, thicker yarns, ribbon, if you can thread it through the eye of a needle you can use it. You pierce the fabric, through the multiple layers to the other side, repeat back through the fabric and then tie it off. It is as simple as it seems and can lead to some really fun results.

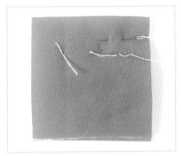

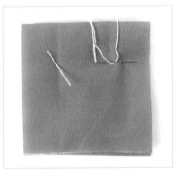

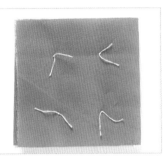

01 Insert needle

Making sure that you are working from the middle outwards, stitch down and back through the layers. Leave a generous tail.

02 Repeat

Now do the same again on the second section.

03 Reef knot

Once you have your placed threads, secure with a reef knot and cut the ends to the same length. Repeat over your project.

Freestyle or free-motion quilting

Freestyle, also known as free-motion, quilting gives machine quilters the same freedom as hand quilters when it comes to the designs on their quilts. With use of a free-motion or darning foot, lower the foot and let your imagination run wild. If your machine has the option to stop work with the needle down, apply it.

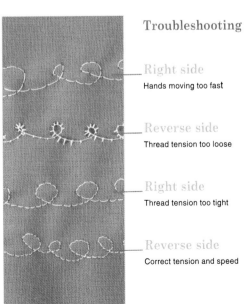

01 First stitches

Make a single stitch and while holding the top threads, pull the bobbin thread to the top. Secure the thread with a few very short stitches. Slowly make a few more stitches. Trim the thread tails.

02 Be free!

With your fingers pressed gentle in a circle around the foot, guide the fabric in any direction of your choosing. Make sure the stitches are the same length, working at a speed you are happy with. Use a few short stitches to tie off when finisihed.

Troubleshooting

Right side
Hands moving too fast

Reverse side
Thread tension too loose

Right side
Thread tension too tight

Reverse side
Correct tension and speed

Embellishing quilts

Take your designs to the next level with some decorative additions

You can make your quilts more interesting to the eye by adding any number of embellishments. These could include surface embroidery and beading to adding buttons, bows and found objects. Whatever kind of embellishment you decide on, always ensure that it actually enhances your design. We've all been seduced by unsuitable bling at some stage!

Buttons

Novelty buttons can be a great way to add charm to theme quilts or folk-art designs. Buttons can also become accent or even 'flowers' at the end of stems in a basket. You can choose the secure the buttons through one or all layers of your quilt, depending on your preference. Buttons are best reserved for decorative pieces like wall hangings or practical things like bags. Be wary that buttons should not be used on quilts for young children and babies as they can become detached.

Charms

Adding small charms to quilts is easy and effective. Tie them in position on the quilt top, depending on the type and size. Charms help add a personal touch. They are best reserved for decorative pieces, though,aw and should not be used on quilts for children and babies, as they too can become choking hazards.

Bows

Tie your bow to the desired size and stitch it in place on the quilt top. Bows can be single or double, but make sure the knot is secure before stitching. If adding bows to a baby quilt, be sure the tail ends are not long enough to present a hazard. Help prevent it from unknotting by stitching a few small stitches through the bow's central knot.

Cording and piping

To give your quilts or cushion covers an extra air of pizazz you can add a decorative edging or cording. Cording is the easiest to apply, you can match it in to your colour, or make it contrast and stand out!

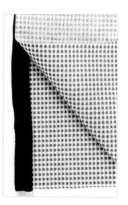

01 Sew the cording

Sew cording between two layers of fabric, like the seamline of a cushion cover, with the right sides together. Align the fabric edge of the cording with the raw edge of the right side of the front piece and tack it in place.

02 Zip foot

Lay the back piece over the cording with the right side facing down. Machine stitch along the outer edge of the cording using a zip foot.

03 Press away

Remove the tacking and turn the fabric the right-side out. Press the fabric away from the cord so that the cord sits neatly along the seamline.

Cover and insert piping cord

01 Set up the bias

Prepare bias strips that are 1½in (4cm) wide. Fold the bias cut fabric strip in half, wrong side to wrong side, over the piping cord, and pin or tack it in place.

02 Stitch to secure

Machine stitch the piping cord in place using either a zip foot or a special piping foot. If the zip foot doesn't run smoothly against the covered cord, tack it in place before machine stitching.

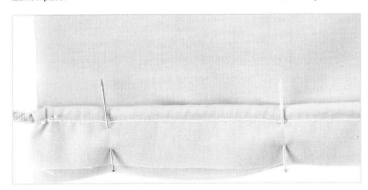

03 Tidy the seam

Trim down the seam allowance on the piping cover so that it is the desired seam allowance width — it can be less than this width but not more. Once you have aligned the piping cover with the intended seamline on the right side of the fabric you can pin it in place. Now tack it together, making sure the piping is facing inwards.

04 Bend and tack

Bend the piping in a 90-degree angle when sewing around a corner. Continue tacking.

05 Pin and sew

Pin the back piece over the front. Using a zip foot, sew the layers together on top of the cord.

06 Finish up

Now turn the piece the right-side out and press the fabric away from the piping.

Fastenings

Ensure your designs aren't ruined by incorrect attachment of fastenings

Fastenings have many practical uses in quilting — securing closings on cushion covers, bags, garments and home accessories — but they can also be used as decoration and adding finishing details. Although they should take second place to the main design, a fastening that has been attached poorly can ruin a project. Use these techniques for successful fastenings.

Sewing on buttons

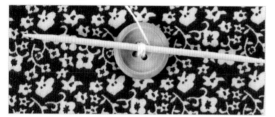

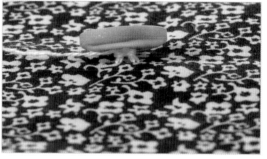

01 Thread over a stick

Using a double strand of thread knotted at the end, pull the needle through the bottom of the fabric to the top where the button will be positioned. Pass the needle through one of the holes in the button and down through another hole to the back. Insert a matchstick or cocktail stick under the stitch so that you don't pull it too tightly. Now pull the thread so it fits snugly around the stick. Continuing working through the holes until you are happy it is secure. Five stitches should do it.

02 Create a shank

Remove the stick. Form a shank by wrapping the working thread around the thread under the button a few times. Secure the thread end with three small stitches at the back of the button.

Hand-stitched buttonholes

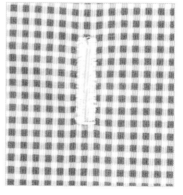

01 Make a mark

Mark the finished length of the buttonhole on the right side of the fabric. Using your machine, stitch a rectangle ¼in (6mm) wide around it. Carefully cut a slit along the exact centre of the rectangle.

02 Stitch around the edge

Use a strong buttonhole thread to work a tailor's buttonhole stitch along both edges of the slit. Be careful to insert the needle through the fabric just outside the machine stitches so that the stitches are ⅛in (3mm) long as you work along.

03 Double up

Stitch to the end of each side, and finish the end with three or four stitches that are the same width as the total width of the buttonhole.

Sew on a zip

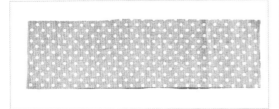

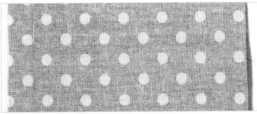

01 Mind the gap

Start by machine stitching a seamline, and leaving a gap in the stitches that is the same length of the zip. The zip will go in this gap.

02 Close up

Tack along the seam line to keep the opening closed.

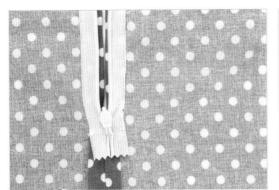

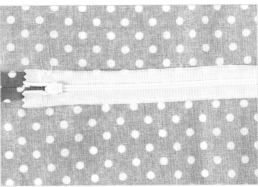

03 Position the zip

Open out the seam and press the seam allowance on the wrong side. Unzip the zip and place it face down on the wrong side of the seam. Making sure the zip's teeth are centred on top of the seam, tack one side of the zip tape in place ⅛in (3mm) from the teeth.

04 Stitch around

Close the zip and tack the other side of the zip tape in place. Machine stitch the zip using matching thread and a zip foot, stitching on the right side of the fabric and forming a rectangle around the zip.

Sew on press studs

05 Remove tacking

Unpick and remove the tacking around the zip tape and along the opening before pressing the edges of the zip.

Make sure the press studs, or poppers, are carefully aligned before sewing them on. Use a double strand of thread and work three or more stitches through each hole around the edge of the press stud pieces.

Projects

Put your new tools and knowledge to the test

130

144

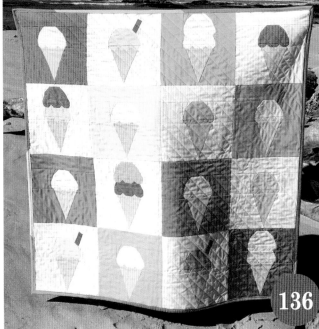

Circuit board quilt

This quilt, inspired by the circuit boards inside our electronics, is perfect for your favourite computer addict — perhaps a teenager glued to his PC?

Name:
Sylvia Schaefer

Bio:
Sylvia Schaefer is a pattern designer and an award-winning quilter. Many of her designs are inspired by science and the natural world.
www.flyingparrotquilts.com

Measurements:
Approximately 50x50in
(127x127cm)

Skills required:
Foundation paper piecing

Seam allowance:
¼" (6.35mm)

Tools and materials:
Foundation paper
Pencil
Ruler
Rotary cutter & mat
Basic sewing supplies

Fabrics used:
Bright green solid:
45in of yardage (144.5cm)
Assorted black prints:
108in of yardage (274cm)
Batting
58x58in **(147.5x147.5cm)**
Backing
117in (297cm)
Binding
18in (46cm)

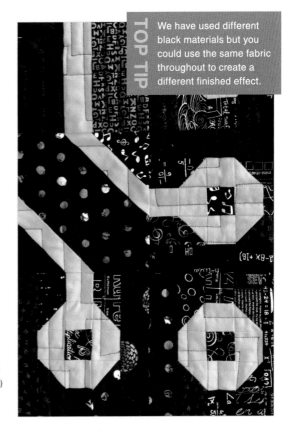

TOP TIP

We have used different black materials but you could use the same fabric throughout to create a different finished effect.

What to cut

From green fabric:
28 rectangles 5.5x1.5in (14x3.5cm)
63 rectangles 5.5x1.25in (14x3cm)
300 squares 1.5x1.5in (3.5x3.5cm)

From assorted black prints:
56 rectangles 5.5x2.5in (14x9cm)
68 rectangles 5.5x1.5in (14x3.5cm)
136 rectangles 2.5x1.5in (9x3 .5cm)
74 squares 1.5x1.5in (3.5x3.5cm)
38 squares 5.75x5.75in (14x14cm)

Get started

01 Make the straight line blocks
Sew a 5.5x1.5in (14x3.5cm) rectangle of black fabric to either side of one of the 5.5x1.5in (14x3.5cm) green rectangles to make 28 straight line blocks. Press the seams towards the black fabric.

02 Prepare the stitch-and-flip triangles
Take 136 of the 1.5x1.5in (3.5x3.5cm) green squares and, using your ruler, draw a line diagonally down the centre of each of the squares.

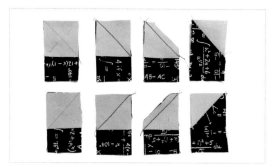

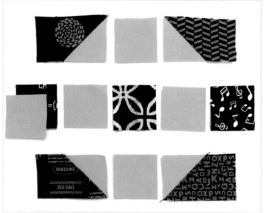

03 Make the stitch-and-flip segments

Align a green square on one end of each 3.5x2in (9x5cm) black rectangle, and stitch along your line. Be certain to alternate the alignment for half (68) of the blocks as shown in the photo. Stitch down the line you marked. Trim the excess from the seam allowance, then press the black fabric away from the triangles.

04 Make rows for the circle blocks

Add a green square between each of two opposite green triangle units. (Make 68 total.) To assemble the centre row, sew together five 2x2in (5x5cm) squares of alternating black and green, with black squares on the outside. On 28 of the blocks, substitute a green square for one of the outside black squares. Make 34 total centre rows.

05 Assemble the circle blocks

Add a stitch-and-flip row to either side of a centre row, then add a 5.5x1.5in (14x3.5cm) strip of black fabric to either side. Press the two centre seams towards the centre and the two outer seams towards the edge. You'll have six stand-alone circles and 28 connected circles.

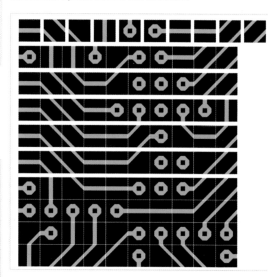

06 Make the foundation paper pieced blocks

Make 38 copies of the Foundation Paper Piecing Template. Using your 5.75x5.75in (14x14cm) black squares and the 5.5x1.5in (14x3.5cm) green strips, piece the blocks following the directions on page 88. Make 25 with all five pieces, and 13 ignoring the dotted lines (it may help to cross them out on your templates to remind you). When trimming the corners off the black squares on your foundation pieced blocks, save the leftover triangles for pieces three and five.

07 Assemble the quilt

Using the assembly diagram above, sew the blocks together in rows. Press seams in opposite directions on each successive row, then sew rows together. To help keep track of the blocks and their orientation, it may help to lay the pieces out on a design wall or your floor.

08 Sandwich, quilt, and bind

Sandwich and quilt, then bind your top. Finish with an all-over free-motion design of square boxes.

TOP TIP

If you are having difficulty aligning the straight and angled blocks, mark a ¼in (6mm) seam allowance on the angled blocks using a wash-out pen and use this line to help you align the green patches.

Wonky weave baby quilt

A playful and airy baby quilt, made with simple techniques

Name:

Stacey Francis

Bio:

Stacey loves designing and making quilts, as well as other patchwork projects. She shares her creations and patterns with everyone who loves quilting or patchwork on her website:

staceyscraftdesigns.com

Measurements:

Approximately 36x48in (90x120cm)

Skills required:

Basic quilting

Log cabin

Seam allowance:

¼in (6mm)

Tools and materials:

Rotary cutter and mat

Quilt ruler(s)

Sewing machine

Thread

Press and board

Hand sewing needle

Fabrics used:

Wonky log cabins and binding:

Pink polka-dot fabric: 18x22in (45x55cm)

Blue polka-dot fabric: 18x22in (45x55cm)

Orange polka-dot fabric: 18x22in (45x55cm)

Purple polka-dot fabric: 18x22in (45x55cm)

Green polka-dot fabric: 18x22in (45x55cm)

Light blue polka-dot fabric: 18x22in (45x55cm)

Rest of top fabric:

Mint/white chevron fabric: 28in in yardage (70x110cm)

Mint/white striped fabric: 28in in yardage (70x110cm)

Batting

The quilt in the picture is made with a low volume bamboo batting

At least 40x52in (100x130cm)

Backing, fabric of choice

At least 40x52in (100x130cm)

What to cut

Cut as you go; uneven/tapered strips of minimal 1in (2.5cm), maximum 2in (5cm) wide, in the length that you need (or longer).

Cut 2 random triangles of each colour (so 12 in total). Make them approximately 2x2in (5x5cm) right-angled triangles.

For the binding cut:

3 strips of 2½x12in (6.5x30cm) of each colour.

If you like to make longer or shorter strips, make sure the total length of your binding is at least 450cm (177in)

Mint/white chevron fabric:

48 4½x4½in (11.5x11.5cm)

Mint/white striped fabric:

48 4½x4½in (11.5x11.5cm)

Get started

01 Uneven/tapered strip one

To sew the wonky log cabin, take 1 triangle and sew an uneven/tapered strip to one side with a ¼in (6mm) seam. Press the seam away from the triangle. Cut the extending piece of uneven/tapered strip in the extension of the triangle edge.

02 Uneven/tapered strip two

Then, sew an uneven/tapered strip to the side where you've just cut of the first uneven/tapered strip with a ¼in (6mm) seam. Press the seam away from the triangle. Cut the extending piece of uneven/tapered strip in the extension of the triangle edge. As you can see the light blue uneven/tapered strip was to short to line the ruler with the edge of the triangle. In that case change the shape of the triangle by cutting off a bit more.

03 Uneven/tapered strip three

Sew (with a ¼in (6mm) seam) an uneven/tapered strip to the side where you've just cut. Press the seam away from the triangle. Cut the extending piece of (pink) uneven/tapered strip in the extension of the other uneven/tapered strip (purple).

04 Sewing around

Continue in the same way on the next side. Always pressing the seams away from the triangle. Keep working your way around, as randomly as you like.

05 Making the wonky log cabin grow

Keep going around and around by adding uneven/tapered strips. Keep in mind you are working towards a square of 4½x4½in (11.5x11.5cm). For easier measuring you can make a paper template in this size. Once your wonky log cabin patch is big enough, you'll need to cut out a square of 4½x4½in (11.5x11.5cm). Repeat Steps 1-4 to create 12 of these in total.

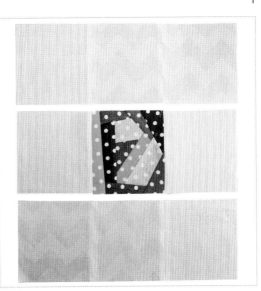

06 Sewing three rows

Lay out the fabric squares as shown above to sew 1 block. Sew the vertical seams with a ¼in (6mm) seam. Press all seams open.

07 Making one block

Sew the horizontal seams with a ¼in (6mm) seam. Make sure to line out the vertical seams. Press all seams open. Make 6 blocks in this layout.

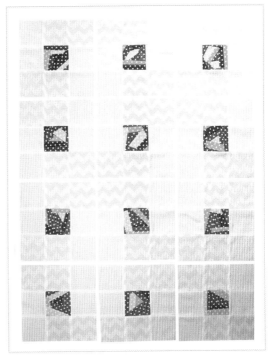

08 Mirrored block B

Make another 6 blocks in the mirrored layout you see above.

09 Sewing 6 rows of blocks

Lay out all the blocks as shown above to create one top. Sew the vertical seams with a ¼in (6mm) seam (see arrows above). Press all seams open.

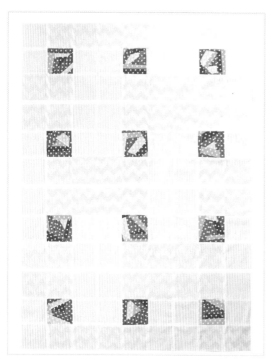

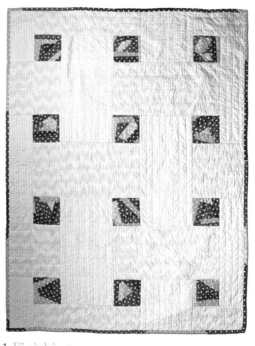

10 Making one top

Sew the horizontal seams with a ¼in (6mm) seam. Make sure to line out all the vertical seams. Press all seams open.

11 Finishing up

Create a quilt sandwich, quilt as you like, square up and add the binding. For this quilt an continuous strip binding was created by sewing by randomly attaching approximately 18 strips of 2½x12in (6.5x30cm) to each other.

TOP TIP

Would you like a bigger (lap size) quilt? Just double the amount of fabric, pieces and blocks from this tutorial!

Crisp cool coasters

Learn to create these simple to make fun coasters with graphic quilt design

Name:
Stacey Francis

Bio:
Stacey loves designing and making quilts, as well as other patchwork projects. She shares her creations and patterns with everyone who loves quilting or patchwork on her website: **staceyscraftdesigns.com**

Measurements:
4x4in (10x10cm)

Skills required:
Basic quilting
Echo quilting

Seam allowance:
¼in (6mm)

Tools and materials:
Rotary cutter and mat
Quilt ruler(s) (cm or inches)
Pencil and ruler
Dissolvable fabric marker
Sewing machine
Thread
Hand sewing needle
Sewing thread in four colours

Fabrics used:

Top and back
Grey: 20x24in (50x60cm)

Bias binding
Blue: 40in (100cm) long
Black and white print: 40in (100cm) long
Green: 40in (100cm) long

Backside cushion, fabric of choice
Two pieces of 26½x32in (66.5x80cm)

Batting
Flannel: 12x20in (30x50cm)

What to cut

Fabric front
6 4¾x4¾in (12x12cm)

Flannel batting
6 5½x5½in (14x14cm)

Fabric back coaster
6 6x6in (5x5cm)

Bias binding
2 20in (50cm) — blue fabric
2 20in (50cm) — black & white fabric
2 20in (50cm) — green

Make cool coasters

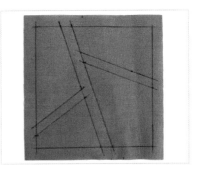

01 Draw square
Draw a square of 4x4in (10x10cm) on the piece of fabric for the front of the coasters. You can use a pencil or other permanent marker as these lines will be covered by the binding.

02 Mark first quilting seam
Draw the first seam lines by using the measurement above or in the style you like. To draw these lines use a dissolvable fabric marker (please test first to make sure the marker does not leave a permanent mark).

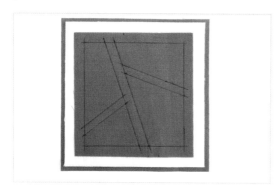

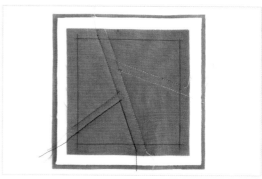

03 Make sandwich

Make a quilt sandwich with the flannel and fabric for the coaster back. As this sandwich is so small and the flannel is not slippery there is no need to pin the layer together. Just make sure you smooth any wrinkles out.

04 Quilt first seams

Make a quilt sandwich with the flannel and fabric for the coaster back. As this sandwich is so small and the flannel is not slippery there is no need to pin the layer together. Just make sure you smooth any wrinkles out.

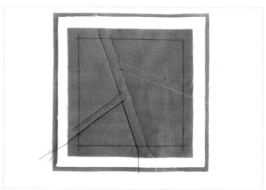

06 Square up

Square up the quilt sandwich to 4x4in (10x10cm).

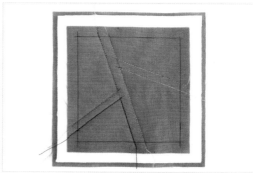

05 Echo quilt

Now the basic shape for the quilting is done, echo quilt in the same colour as the first seam. With echo quilting you use a seam to guide the edge of a ¼in (6mm) or a basic sewing foot to create echoing seams. Above both sewing foot sizes were used to give the coaster a more interesting appeal.

07 Finished coaster back

Add the bias binding by using the technique. Above you can see the backside of the coaster with the bias binding attached with a blind seam.

Topsy-turvy cushion cover

A great big comfy cushion to chill on

Name:

Stacey Francis

Bio:

Stacey loves designing and making quilts, as well as other patchwork projects. She shares her creations and patterns with everyone who loves quilting or patchwork on her website: **staceyscraftdesigns.com**

Measurements:

Approximately 26x26in (60x60cm)

Skills required:

Basic quilting

String piecing

Seam allowance:

¼in (6mm)

Tools and materials:

Rotary cutter and mat

Quilt ruler(s)

Sewing machine

Thread

Iron and board

Dissolvable fabric marker

Fabrics used:

Top; X designs

Dark red solid fabric: 4x18in (10x45cm)

Red print fabric: 4x18in (10x45cm)

Dark orange solid fabric: 4x18in (10x45cm)

Orange print fabric: 4x18in (10x45cm)

Top; grey background fabric

Grey fabric 1: 16x14in (40x35cm)

Grey fabric 2: 16x14in (40x35cm)

Grey fabric 3: 16x14in (40x35cm)

Grey fabric 4: 16x14in (40x35cm)

Grey fabric 5: 16x14in (40x35cm)

Batting

30x30in (75x75cm)

Backing, fabric of choice (inside of cushion)

30x30in (75x75cm)

Backside cushion, fabric of choice

Two pieces of 26½in × 32in (66.5x80cm)

What to cut

Cut 3 strips in the following sizes in each of the 5 grey fabrics

1⅛x14in (3x35cm)

1⅝x14in (4x35cm)

2x14in (5x35cm)

You should have 54 strips in total

Cut 2 strips of 2x18in (5x45cm) per colour.

TOP TIP

If you like a more colourful cushion, you can use more exuberant colours as background fabric and a contrasting or neutral colour for the X shapes.

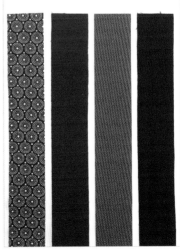

Get started

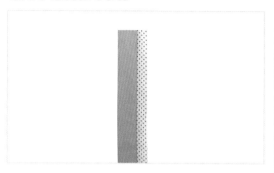

01 Go random

Sew the grey strips together, in random fabric style and width, to make the striped grey background base for the X blocks. Use a ¼in (6mm) seam and iron the seam in one direction. Continue sewing together strips in this random fabric style and width. Make sure you vary the width throughout. Keep on ironing the seams in one direction.

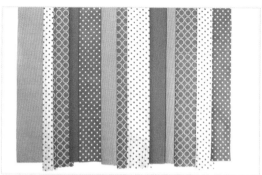

02 Measure the progress

Once you've sewn approximately 13 strips together your piece should be 14in (35cm) wide, so have a check of the size. If your piece is smaller, simply add another strip.

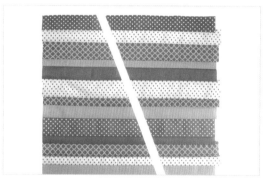

03 Slash diagonally

Lay the grey background piece on your cutting mat with the grey strips in a horizontal direction (as shown above). Place your ruler in a diagonal angle that you like and then cut the piece diagonally.

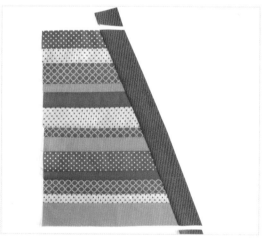

04 Piece the first half of an X

Sew one of the red/orange strips to the diagonal rough edge you've just cut (with a ¼in (6mm) seam). Make sure you don't stretch the grey fabric too much, because it's cut on the bias (diagonally), so it tends to stretch more. Iron the seam towards the red/orange fabric. Cut the extending red/orange fabric strips in line with the grey fabric edge.

05 Finish the first X half

Now, flip over the other grey background half and line out the raw edge of the diagonal cut with the edge of the red/orange fabric. Make sure you line out the top and bottom ¼in (6mm) inwards of the edge. Sew with a ¼in (6mm) seam. Iron the seam towards the red/orange fabric. The image on the left shows what the finished X half looks like.

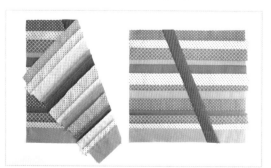

06 Slash a different diagonal

Lay the grey background piece on your cutting mat with the grey strips in a vertical direction (as shown above) and place your ruler at a different diagonal angle. Cut the piece diagonally.

07 Piece the second X half

Sew the second of the red/orange strips to the rough edge of the diagonal you just cut (with a ¼in (6mm) seam). Make sure you don't stretch the grey fabric too much. Iron the seam towards the red/orange fabric. Make two marks (with appropriate dissolvable fabric marker, please test first to make sure it does not leave any permanent marks on your fabric) in extension of the first X half (see anno above).

08 Sew the second X half

Flip over the other grey background half and line out the raw edge of the diagonal cut with the edge of the red/orange fabric. Take care to ensure you line out the other half of the first X with the marks you made. Sew with a ¼in (6mm) seam. Iron the seam towards the red/orange fabric.

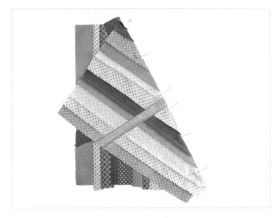

09 Squaring up

Cut out a square of 34cm × 34cm (13½in × 13½in). Make sure the vertical lines of the grey strips are perpendicular to the sides.

10 Finished block

This is what a finished block looks like. Make four blocks in total, each one with its own red or orange X in it.

Top assembly

11 Piece two blocks together

Lay out the four blocks in a composition you like, making sure to alternate the vertical and horizontal direction of the grey stripes. Sew together the two vertical seams with a ¼in (6mm) seam. Iron the seam away from the vertical grey strip seams.

12 Sew four blocks together

Next, sew the horizontal seam, making sure you nest the vertical middle seam (see circle, right). See page 54 on set-in seams. Iron this seam open.

Open piece

Folded piece

13 Create sandwich and quilt

Create a quilt sandwich, and then quilt as you like.

14 Create the cushion back

To create the envelope back of the cushion cover, take the two fabric pieces of 26½in × 32in (66.5cm × 80cm), fold crosswise and iron the fold.

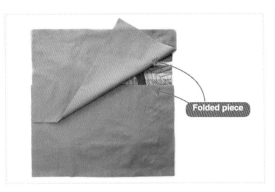

Folded piece

15 Position over the design

Lay the two folded pieces on the right side of the quilted top. Make sure the raw edges line out with the edge of the quilted top and the folds point towards the middle.

16 Allow for constriction

Pin all around. The fabric for the back of the cushion might seem too large but the quilted top tends to constrict a bit, so stretch the quilt sandwich and line out with the edge of the back fabric.

17 Sew the seam

Sew with a generous ¼in (6mm) seam all around and trim the corners. Turn inside out and your cushion cover is finished.

TOP TIP

If you wanted to you could use buttons to hold your cushion back closed, adding fun buttons for an extra feature.

Alhambra lap quilt

This quilt was inspired by the Moorish tiles found in the Alhambra Palace

Name:
Stacey Francis

Bio:
Stacey loves designing and making quilts, as well as other patchwork projects. She shares her creations and patterns with everyone who loves quilting or patchwork on her website: **staceyscraftdesigns.com**

Measurements:
Approximately 51x71in (130x80cm)

Skills required:
Basic quilting
String piecing
Flying geese

Seam allowance:
¼in (6mm)

Tools and materials:
Rotary cutter and mat
Fabric scissors
Quilt ruler(s) (cm or inches)
Pencil and ruler
Sewing machine
Thread
Press and board
Hand sewing needle

Fabrics used:
Top; dots
Green: 20x44in (50x110cm)
Petrol: 20x44in (50x110cm)
Blue: 20x44in (50x110cm)
Yellow: 20x44in (50x110cm)
Dark blue: 20x44in (50x110cm)

Top; background fabric
Light grey: 79x44in (200x110cm)

Batting of choice
At least 55x75in (140x190cm)

Backing, fabric of choice
At least 55x75in (140x190cm)

Binding, medium grey
28½in of yardage (72x110cm)

What to cut

In yellow, blue, petrol, green and dark blue cut
22x1½x1½in (56x4x4cm) (flying geese)
33x2½x2½in (84x6.5x6.5cm)
5.5x3x3in (14x7.5x7.5cm) (half square triangles)

Background fabric
148x2½x2½in (376x6.5x6.5cm)
27x3x3in (70x7.5x7.5cm) (half square triangles)

Binding
6 strips of 4¾in yardage (12x110cm)

Overview of all the blocks

This shows all the blocks you need to sew. Either sew all the half square triangles and extended flying geese squares in one go, or sew the ones you need per block to create more variation in your workflow.

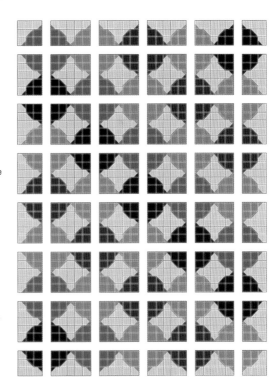

Construct a stunning blanket

01 Make half square triangle

Make 28 of each colour combination you see above. See page 32 on how to make half square triangles with two rectangles.

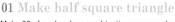

02 Make extended flying geese square

Make 14 of each colour combination you see above. See page 61 on how to make flying geese. To make these extended flying geese, you'll use the 2½x2½in (6.5x6.5cm) background fabric squares instead of rectangles.

03 Make 'half' extended flying geese square

Make the amounts in the colour combination you see above. Make these in the same way as Step 2, with only one triangle.

04 Sew three rows

Lay out the fabric squares as shown above to sew one corner block. Check the schedule on the previous page for the colour combinations you have to sew. Sew the vertical seams with a ¼in (6mm) seam. Press all seams open.

05 Make one corner block

Sew the horizontal seams with a ¼in (6mm) seam. Make sure that you line out the vertical seams (see page 39 on how to line out open seams). Press all seams open.

TOP TIP

If you didn't want to create a uniform look to your quilt, you could also arrange the dots randomly instead of the diagonal stripes used in this design.

06 Finished corner block

This is what one corner block looks like. Make the other three corner blocks in the colour combinations shown on page 135.

07 Sew five rows

Lay out the fabric squares as shown above to sew one edge block. Sew the vertical seams with a ¼in (6mm) seam and then press all seams open.

08 Make one edge block

Sew the horizontal seams with a ¼in (6mm) seam. Make sure to line out the vertical seams. Press all seams open.

09 Finished edge block

This is what one edge block looks like. Make the other 19 edge blocks.

10 Build up a block

Lay out the fabric squares as shown above to sew one full block. Sew the vertical seams with a ¼in (6mm) seam. Press all seams open.

12 Finished full block

Once you have finished, make the other 23 full blocks.

11 Make one full block

Sew the horizontal seams with a ¼in (6mm) seam. Make sure to line out the vertical seams. Press all seams open.

13 How to sew sets of six blocks

To create one top, lay out all the blocks. To keep the sewing manageable, sew these blocks together into sets of six. First sew the vertical seams to create two rows of three blocks (with a ¼in (6mm) seam). Make sure you line out all the horizontal seams. Then sew these two rows together with a ¼in (6mm) seam. Make sure you line out all the vertical seems. Press all the seams open to prevent bulk fabric.

14 Sew four parts

Sew the previously sewn eight parts into four parts by sewing the four horizontal seams with a ¼in (6mm) seam. Make sure you line out all the vertical seams. Press all seams open.

15 Sew two parts

Sew the previously sewn eight parts into four parts by sewing the four horizontal seams with a ¼in (6mm) seam. Make sure you line out all the vertical seams. Press all seams open.

16 Make one top

Sew the previously sewn two parts into one top by sewing the last horizontal seam with a ¼in (6mm) seam. Press all seams open.

TOP TIP

You could add freeform quilting to the pattern in the grey sections of the fabric for a varied finished look.

17 Finish up

To complete, create a quilt sandwich — quilt as you like — square up and add the binding. For this quilt, an extra wide bias binding was created by using 6 strips of 6 strips of 4¾in yardage (12x110cm).

Ice cream beach blanket

This is the perfect project to make on a warm summer's day — cheery ice cream, but without the calories! Make it with solids, or find some great textured prints to really add detail

Name:
Kristy Lea

Bio:
While Kristy loves to quilt, her heart belongs to foundation piecing. She loves to both make and create. She has been designing and selling foundation-pieced patterns on various themes in her shop since 2012.
payhip.com/quietplay

Measurements:
Block size: 10in (25cm)
Quilt size: is 40x40in (100cm)

Skills required:
Foundation piecing

Seam allowance:
¼in (6mm) for all seams

Tools and materials:
Foundation paper (or cheap printer paper)
Thread
Scissors
Rotary cutter and mat

Fabrics used:

Front
54in of yardard (137cm) in white
8 fat quarters in pink, blue, yellow, light green, dark green, orange, teal and purple
18in of yardage (46cm) beige for ice cream cones
5 fat eighths for other ice cream colours — mint, chocolate, strawberry, banana and bubblegum

Batting
50x50in (127x127cm)

Backing
50x50in (127x127cm)

Binding
15in width of fabric (38cm) — or use the leftover colours from your quilt to make a scrappy batting

---

What to cut

Cutting requirements are guidelines and will be larger than required — expect to have scraps left over!

Single scoop
You will make three single-scoop blocks with a white background, and five with a coloured background. Refer to the chart (right) for colour patterns.

For section A (cone)
From the background fabric, cut two squares measuring 6x6in (15x15cm).
From the beige cone fabric, cut a rectangle measuring 4x7in (10x18cm)

For section B (scoop)
From the background fabric, cut a rectangle measuring 11x3in (28x7.5cm), two small rectangles measuring 2x4in (5x10cm) and two squares measuring 4x4in (10x10cm).
From the ice cream fabric, cut a rectangle measuring 3x5in (7.5x12.5cm). Cut a strip measuring 2x10in (5x25cm).

From the beige cone fabric, cut a strip measuring 2x10in (5x25cm).

Double scoop
You will make two double-scoop blocks with a white background, and two with a coloured background.

For section A (cone)
As single scoop.

For section B (bottom scoop)
From the background fabric, cut two small rectangles measuring 2x4in (5x10cm). Cut a strip measuring 2x10in (5x25cm).
For the ice cream and cone fabric see single scoop.

For section C (top scoop)
From the background fabric, cut two squares measuring 4x4in (10x10cm). Cut a strip measuring 2x10in (5x25cm).
From the ice cream fabric, cut a rectangle measuring 3x3.5in (7.5x9cm). Cut a strip measuring 2x10in (5x25cm).

Chocolate flake
You will make three ice cream flake blocks with a white background, and one with a coloured background.

For section A (cone) and B cone)
As single scoop.

For section C (chocolate flake)
From the chocolate fabric, cut one rectangle measuring 1.5x3in (3.75x7.5cm).
From the background fabric, cut 3 3.5x6.5in (9x16.5cm). Cut a strip measuring 2x10in (5x25cm).

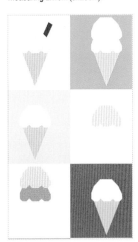

Create a flurry of flavours

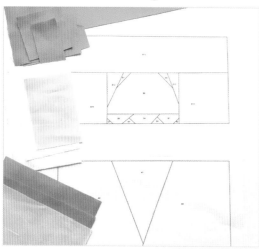

01 Print your templates

Print or photocopy a total of 16 ice cream cone templates (Section B). Print or photocopy eight single-scoop templates, four double-scoop templates and four chocolate flake templates (Sections B and C). Repeat with Section B to make the top of the ice cream.

03 Sew the single-scoop block together

Join Section A to Section B. Use pins to hold the two pieces in place, and sew with the smaller stitch length. Remove the paper from the seam allowance. Iron your completed block well.

Repeat this step to make all eight single-scoop blocks. Make three blocks on a white background with ice cream flavours of bubblegum, strawberry and melon. Make five vanilla ice creams with background colours of pink, yellow, teal, orange and light green.

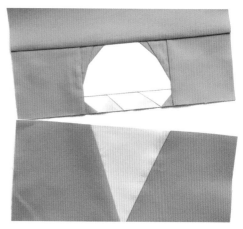

02 Piece the single-scoop block

Using the foundation-piecing technique (see page 84), sew Section A of the templates to make the cone. Make sure you press the seams well. Trim Section A back to the seam allowance. Repeat with Section B to make the top of the ice cream.

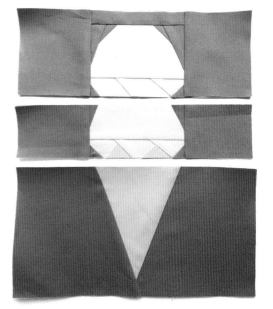

04 Piece the double-scoop block

Using the foundation-piecing technique (see page 84), again sew Section A of the templates to make the cone, making sure that you press the seams well. Trim Section A back to the seam allowance. Repeat with Sections B and C to make the top of the ice cream.

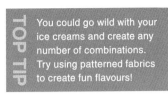
You could go wild with your ice creams and create any number of combinations. Try using patterned fabrics to create fun flavours!

05 Sew the double-scoop block together

Join Section B to Section C. Then join Section A to Sections BC. Use pins to hold the two pieces in place, and sew with the smaller stitch length. Remove the paper from the seam allowance. Iron your completed block well. Repeat this step to make all four double-scoop blocks. Make two blocks on a white background with ice cream flavours of chocolate + mint and strawberry + chocolate. Make two vanilla ice creams with background colours of blue and purple.

06 Piece the ice cream flake block

As previously, use the foundation-piecing technique (see page 84) and sew Section A of the templates to make the cone. Make sure you press the seams well, then trim Section A back to the seam allowance. Repeat with Sections B and C to make the top of the ice cream.

07 Sew the ice cream flake block together

Join Section B to Section C. Then join Section A to Sections BC. Use pins to hold the two pieces in place, and sew with the smaller stitch length. Remove the paper from the seam allowance. Iron your completed block well. Repeat this step to make all four ice cream flake blocks. Make three blocks on a white background with ice cream flavours of mint, banana and strawberry. Make one vanilla ice cream with a background colour of green.

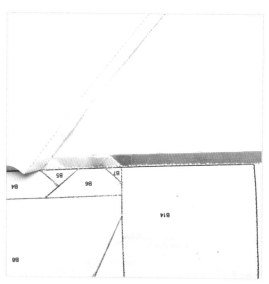

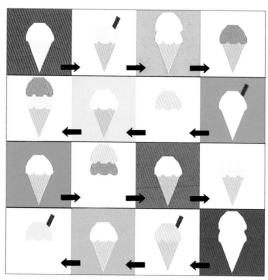

08 Remove the papers

Remove the foundation paper from all of the blocks. Be careful not to pull too hard and stretch the seams. Press the blocks well.

09 Join the blocks together

Following the layout above, join your blocks together in rows. Press each rows' seams in alternating directions as shown on the diagram. This is so that when you join the rows together, the seams will nest nicely and you will have tidy seams where the blocks meet.

10 Baste the quilt

Baste your quilt ready for quilting. You can use a wideback fabric for the backing of this quilt, or piece one together to make it large enough to fit.

11 Quilt as desired

Quilt your quilt sandwich in your preferred manner. For diagonal quilting like on this quilt, you will need to mark one long diagonal line from point to point. A Hera marker is perfect for this as it will leave a crease mark on your quilt for you to follow with your walking foot.

Change your stitch length to 4.0 and trace the first line from corner to corner. Using a guide on your walking foot, follow the first quilting line, quilting straight lines 1.5in apart.

12 Bind your quilt

You can use leftover fabric from your quilt to create a scrappy binding as shown in this quilt. Using your preferred method, complete your quilt with binding. Remember to add in a label to finish off your quilt.

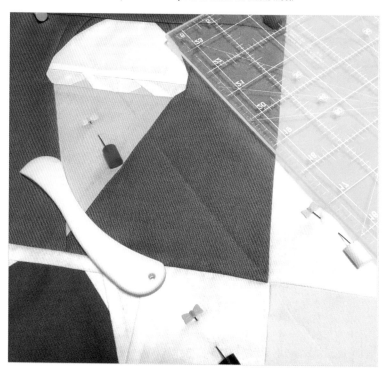

TOP TIP

Remove the paper from the
seam allowances as you join
sections of your block. Your
block will lay flatter, and you
won't need to remove tiny pieces
of paper caught in seams.

Diamonds and more tote bag

A lovely big bag with a foundation paper piecing accent in the middle

Name:

Stacey Francis

Bio:

Stacey loves designing and making quilts, as well as other patchwork projects. She shares her creations and patterns with everyone who loves quilting or patchwork on her website: **staceyscraftdesigns.com**

Measurements:

Approximately 16½inx14½inx5½in (42cmx37cmx14cm)

Skills required:

Basic quilting
Foundation paper piecing

Seam allowance:

¼in (6mm)

Tools and materials:

Rotary cutter and mat
Quilt ruler(s)
Sewing machine
Thread
Iron and board
Computer & printer or copier
Scissors or paper cutting knife

Fabrics used:

Outside bag

Print fabric A: diamond fabric: 18×18in (45x45cm)

Print fabric B: medium blue (solid) fabric: 5×18in (12x45cm)

Print fabric C: yellow (flowers) fabric: 5×18in (12x45cm)

Background fabric: grey: 18×18in (45x45cm)

Dark blue (polka dot) fabric: 28×19½in (72cmx50cm)

Inside bag (backing of quilting part)

Medium blue (polka dot) fabric at least 22x22in (55x55cm)

Bias binding top edge

Print fabric B: medium blue (solid) fabric or ready-bought bias binding, length 40in (100cm)

Optional bias binding inside bag

Flannel at least 22x22in (55x55cm)

Batting

Flannel at least 22x22in (55x55cm)

Straps

(Nylon) purse strap webbing 2 1x61in (2.5x155cm)

What to cut

Print fabric A

11x2x4in (28cmx6cmx10cm) rectangle cut diagonally (14 in one direction and 14 in the other direction)

Print fabric B

5½x1x4in (14cmx3cmx11cm)

Print fabric C

5½x1x4in (14cmx3cmx11cm)

Background fabric

22x1x4in (56cmx3cmx11cm)

For the dark blue (polka dot) sides

1½x7x19½in (4cmx18cmx50cm)

> **TOP TIP**
>
> If you don't fancy doing the foundation paper piecing panel, you can use a patterned piece of fabric (6x19½in (15.5x50cm)) to replace the foundation paper piecing panel.

Foundation paper piecing

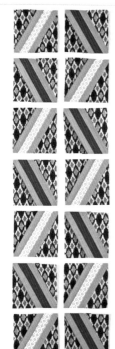

01 Foundation paper piecing

Print or copy the foundation paper piecing template on page 165 seven times (make sure your printer or copier is set to 100%). Use the technique described on page 88 to make these foundation paper pieces.

02 Piecing the FPP

Lay out 14 FPP pieces as shown on the left. (7 template A and 7 template B pieces). Sew the vertical seams with a ¼in (6mm) seam. Iron the seams open.

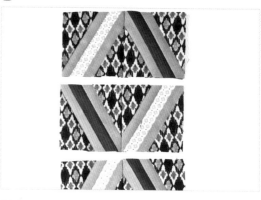

03 Piecing the FPP

Sew the horizontal seams with a ¼in (6mm) seam. Make sure you line out all the vertical and diagonal seams. Iron the seams open.

04 Create two FPP pieces

Repeat Steps 2 and 3 with the other 14 FPP pieces to create the second FPP panel.

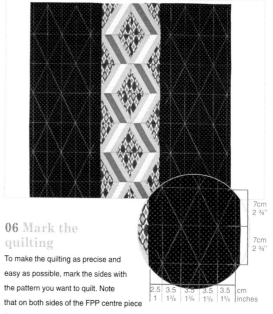

06 Mark the quilting

To make the quilting as precise and easy as possible, mark the sides with the pattern you want to quilt. Note that on both sides of the FPP centre piece

| 2.5 | 3.5 | 3.5 | 3.5 | 3.5 | cm |
| 1 | 1³⁄₈ | 1³⁄₈ | 1³⁄₈ | 1³⁄₈ | inches |

7cm 2 ¾"

7cm 2 ¾"

05 Attach the sides

Attach two of the dark blue (polka dot) fabric pieces to the FPP panel with a ¼in (6mm) seam. Iron the seams towards the dark blue (polka dot) fabric. Repeat with the other two dark blue (polka dot) fabric pieces and FPP panel to create the second 'bag top'.

the straps will be attached, so your seams won't be visible here. Above you can see that the 1in (2.5in) beside the FPP panel is not going to be quilted. The vertical lines above have a distance of 15/8in (3.5cm) and the horizontal lines are in line with the horizontal seams in the FPP centre piece. Draw a diagonal line where the horizontal and vertical lines intersect to create diamond shapes.

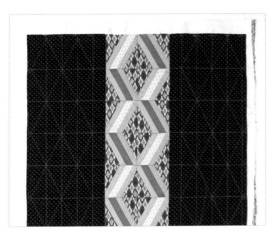

07 Create quilt sandwich and quilt

Create a quilt sandwich with the flannel and backing fabric (medium blue (polka dot)). This bag was quilted by sewing the vertical and horizontal seams of the FPP panel as well as around the diamond shapes. The sides were quilted with the previously drawn pattern (see Step 6). Repeat this step and the next with the other bag top, to create the other quilted half of the bag.

08 Squaring up

Square up both of the bag halves. The edge of the top should work as your guide.

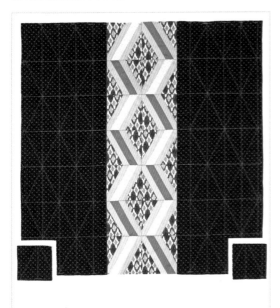

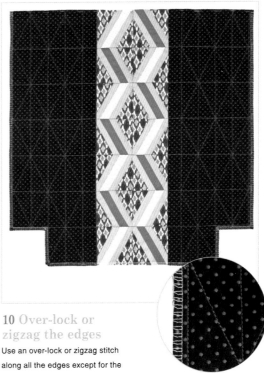

09 Cut out corner squares for 3D corners

Lay out one of the squared-up bag halves (with the full diamond in the middle, upwards). Cut away a 2¾x2¾in (7x7cm) square at both of the bottom corners. Repeat with the other bag half, make sure you lay this half with the full diamond upwards as well.

10 Over-lock or zigzag the edges

Use an over-lock or zigzag stitch along all the edges except for the top. Repeat with the other bag half.

11 Add binding to the top

Add bias binding to the top of both bag halves. See page 42 on how to
add bias binding.

12 Sew the straps

Line out the strap from the bottom edge along the side of the FPP panel
upwards, repeat with the other half. Now, you should have a loop at the
top. Make sure the loop is not twisted. Sew the straps and then repeat
with the other bag half.

13 Sew sides and bottom

Lay the two bag halves with the right side (outside) together.
Pin in place and sew the sides and bottom.

14 Sewing the corners

Pull the two bag halves apart at the inside
corners of the 'gap' at the bottom corner. Line
out the two sides, nest the seam and pin. Repeat
with the other side of the bag.

15 Check the seams

Make sure the side and bottom seams (see arrows — these are with
bias binding) face away from each other.

TOP TIP

If you want to make the inside of the bag extra polished, add bias binding to the seams.

Reference

All the technical stuff you need in one handy place

"A big part of making your quilt is deciding on the patchwork (and possibly even the backing!)"

Patchwork block gallery

These are some of the most common ways to put patchwork together

A big part of making your quilt is deciding on the patchwork pattern you want to go on your quilt top (and possibly even your backing). There are so many different ways to patchwork, we can't possibly cover them all here. But by mastering a few of these basics, you'll find that you're able to recognise how patchwork patterns you like the look of are put together, and recreating them yourself will be easy. For your first patchwork quilt pattern, we recommend trying something quite easy, as that way you'll be able to focus on mastering the techniques, instead of getting bogged down in the detail.

Four-patch blocks

Putting four squares together forms a four-patch block. The four blocks you put together can be simple squares, or can be made up of a number of other pieces to make an intricate pattern.

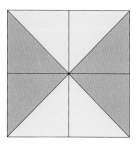
Yankee puzzle

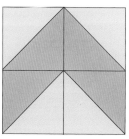
Chevron or Streak of lightning

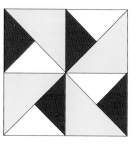
Broken pinwheel

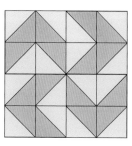
Flyfoot

Five and seven-patch blocks

These have a slightly misleading name when compared to the four and nine-patch blocks, as the numbers on these reference the amount of squares in each direction, not in total. Therefore, a five-patch block will have 25 squares and a seven-patch block will have 49. With so many squares to place, the combinations are almost endless.

Star and cross patch

Duck and ducklings

Hens and chickens

Dove in a window

Nine-patch blocks

Probably the most common way to put patchwork together is with the nine-patch blocks pattern, in which the squares are laid out simply in three rows of three blocks.

Pictorial blocks

These types of blocks are an opportunity to express your creativity, and make a stylised pattern of your own choosing by using square and triangle units in different combinations.

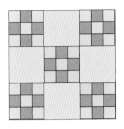

Red cross-Three-colour nine-patch   Three-colour double nine-patch

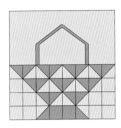

Grape basket   Colonial basket

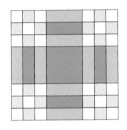

Rocky road to California   Building blocks

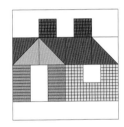

Basket of scraps   House with fence

Strip-pieced blocks

Squares made up of strips can yield really interesting patterns, including basketweaves and chevrons. They're also great for creating pieced border strips.

Log cabin blocks

Named after a traditional patchwork that used a warm colour in the centre to represent a hearth and then built around it, the variations offered by using light and dark colours in this block can create striking geometric patterns.

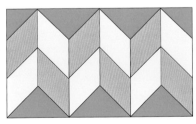

Double chevron seminole

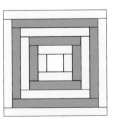
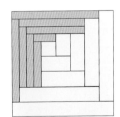

Cabin in the cotton   Thick and thin

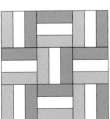

Basketweave   String-pieced divided square

Chimneys and cornerstones   Pineapple

Star blocks

Star blocks are a classic way to put patchwork together and are always stunning to look at. There are many ways to put a star block together, ranging from simple four-square blocks to intricate, complex designs.

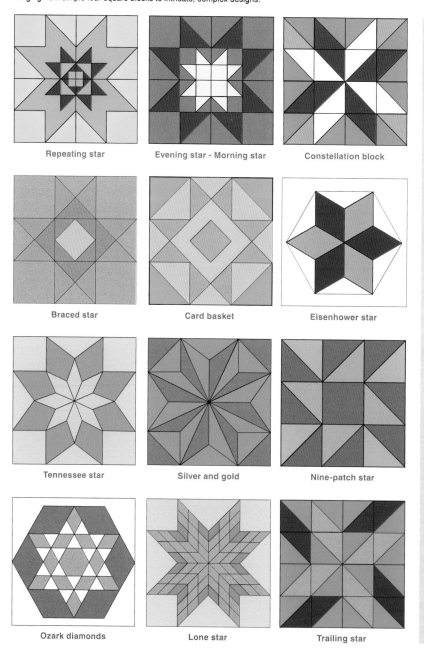

Repeating star

Evening star - Morning star

Constellation block

Braced star

Card basket

Eisenhower star

Tennessee star

Silver and gold

Nine-patch star

Ozark diamonds

Lone star

Trailing star

Tips for making blocks

Measure twice, cut once

Always double check all of your measurements before you begin cutting, as once you start, it's too late to go back. It's also good practice to use the same ruler for everything in one project, as different ones may have slightly different markings.

Sew a bias edge to a straight edge

Try to do this wherever possible, as this will minimise the risk of the piece stretching due to the nature of fabric cut on the bias.

Make a measuring block

Start off by making a very simple block that is the size that you want all the rest to be. Then, when you finish a patterned one, you can then use the guide block to check its size.

Trim all sides equally

If you find that you have made a block too big, make sure to trim it from each side equally, instead of just taking all of the excess off one side. This will ensure your pattern stays centred.

Curved blocks

Adding curves is a fairly complex technique, but by using multiple colours, orientations and sizes of curve, the results you can achieve can be really quite intricate and beautiful. You can make curved blocks of any size, from four-patch to seven-patch.

Mosaic blocks

These are traditionally hand sewn using the English paper-piecing method. Using a mosaic gives you an opportunity to create a motif that isn't necessarily symmetrical.

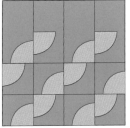

Falling timbers

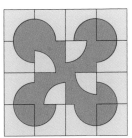

Wonder of the world

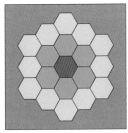

Grandmother's flower garden

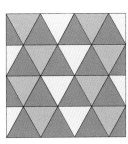

1000 pyramids

Chain links

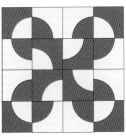

Drunkard's puzzle

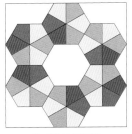

Tumbling blocks

Flower basket

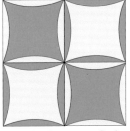

Robbing Peter to pay Paul

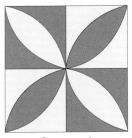

Orange peel

Fan blocks

Create fans by using quarter circles, which can either be pointed or curved. They are usually applied by appliqué to a background, which you can then either let show through or completely hide, and will create a curving pattern.

Dresden plate

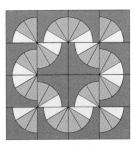

Mohawk trail

Quilt layouts

Form a design for your quilt to make it as creative as possible

A straight set

The simplest technique to set your quilt is to opt for repeating blocks that are stitched together from edge to edge.

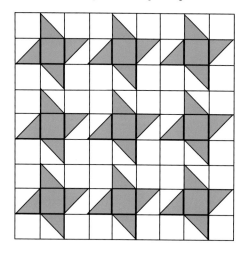

Alternating blocks

If time is of the essence, put half as many blocks together as you need, and alternate between a patterned block and a plain one. This is also a great set if you want to showcase more elaborate elements, as the plain elements won't detract from the detail.

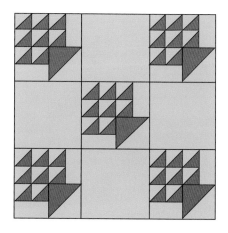

Blocks on point

To achieve a slightly more creative result, you can turn the blocks at an angle, so that the points of each square are touching. This is called 'on point'. You'll need to set triangles at the edges.

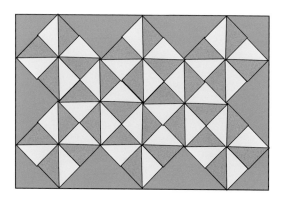

Alternating pieced and plain

Place your pieced blocks alongside each other on point with the corners touching, and fill in the gaps with plain patches. You'll need triangular patches along the edges.

Log cabin blocks

There are plenty of ways to style log cabin sets. Ultimately, all log cabin sets are made up of identically sized pieces of material and arranged in different ways to achieve a unique final result.

Light and dark

Barn raising

Straight furrow

Medallion set

Named for its central element, the medallion setting (also known as the frame setting) is done by building on borders of various width.

Strippy set

To achieve the popular strippy set, you'll want to arrange your blocks vertically on strips that connect to form with width of the quilt.

Rotating set

Set one block in an asymmetrical style and then repeat, rotating each set to create a unique pattern.

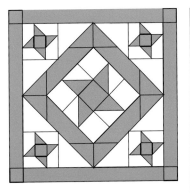

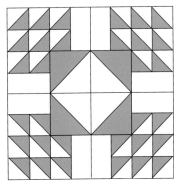

Templates

Helpful guides for your quilting projects

Log cabin 13 step guide:
(see page 82)

Circuit board quilt:
(see page 110-113) Size: 75%

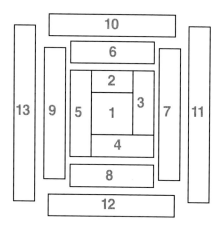

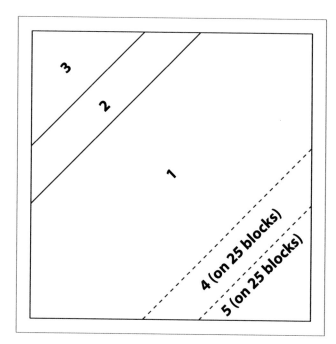

Ice cream beach blanket: Single scoop:

(see page 136-141) Size: 75%

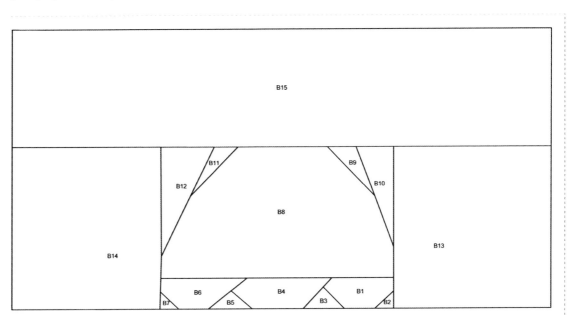

Ice cream beach blanket: Ice cream cone:

(see page 136-141) Size: 75%

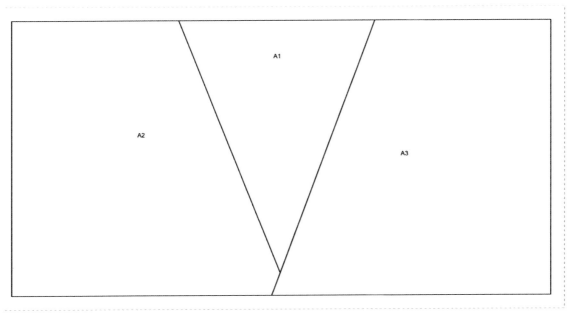

Ice cream beach blanket: Double scoop:
(see page 136-141) Size: 75%

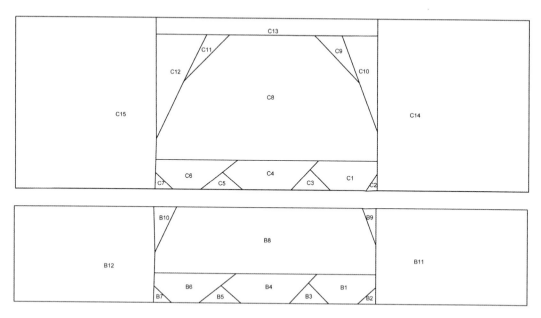

Ice cream beach blanket: Single scoop with flake:
(see page 140-145) Size: 75%

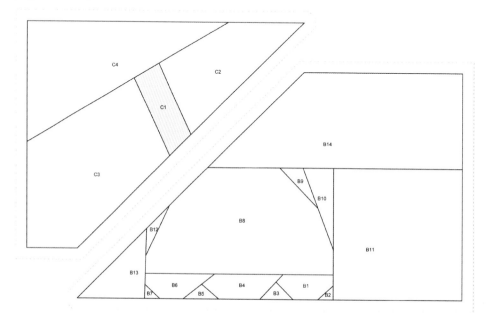

Diamonds and more tote bag:

(see page 142-147) Actual size

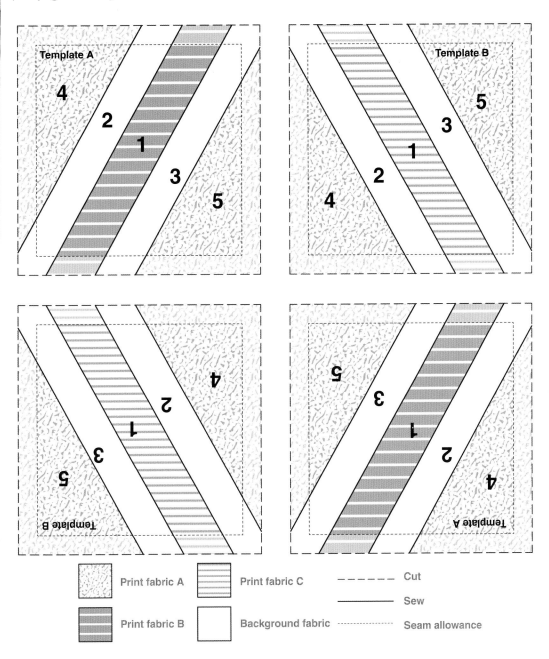

Template A

Template B

Template B

Template A

Print fabric A	Print fabric C	— — — — — Cut
Print fabric B	Background fabric	—————— Sew
		············ Seam allowance